PATRICK LEVI SWEENEY

From cabin boy to ship's captain in the golden age of sail.

CAPTAIN BOB CERULLO

AuthorHouse™
1663 Liberty Drive
Bloomington, IN 47403
www.authorhouse.com
Phone: 833-262-8899

This book is printed on acid-free paper.

ISBN: 979-8-8230-3037-3 (sc)
ISBN: 979-8-8230-3038-0 (e)

Library of Congress Control Number: 2024914815

Print information available on the last page.

Published by AuthorHouse 08/06/2024

authorHOUSE®

Contents

*This book is gratefully dedicated
to my friend Marie Connor.*

Patrick Levi Sweeney was my great-grandfather who passed away long before I was born. Nonetheless he was my hero. I learned what I know of him from long conversations with my mother, his granddaughter. Evenings after dinner, I would sit at the kitchen table and chat while my mom related to me the tales of Patrick Sweeney told to her by her mother and grandmother. As a boy of eight years or so I was so inspired by the stories that I became the captain of my ship, which was our back porch. My dad had attached a real boat helm to the railing and my mother contributed a sheet to be my mainsail. I sailed my fantasy ship over an ocean of backyard grass with my first mate, my dog Scotty, at my side. In my fantasy as a master of the sailing ship Invincible, I vanquished my boyhood pal Blackbeard George the pirate several times. This, then, is my recollection of those stories, research from cemetery records, and my conception of what was likely to have occurred. It is a sort of biographical novel about an interesting man I am privileged to call my great-grandfather. This historical novel then, is my effort to tell the story of Patrick Levi Sweeney in what might have been his own words.

Port Huron, Ohio is the place where it all began for me. My mother told me that I was born on a beautiful day in late October of 1841 on our farm at the edge of town. She said the leaves had turned their rainbow of vivid colors. The midwife, Mrs. O'Connell, and her daughter Constance arrived at just the right time, Mom said. I guess I was about two months old when I was baptized Patrick Levi Sweeney by a Catholic priest in town. Mom had a picture of me when I was baptized. I was wearing a very fancy white dress. I hated that picture and was glad it was kept hidden away someplace.

Fortunately, our home was located a short distance from the town, yet on the edge of our farm. Ours was a large dairy farm with some fifty cows which kept my mom and dad busy from morning until night. Just like my brother John and darling sister Bertha Kate, I was put to work milking just as soon as I had enough strength to squeeze a cow's teat. The aroma of the barn became very much a part of my life. I was eager to learn, which I soon discovered was a mistake, because there seemed to be no end to the cows that needed milking. I was about eight years old when I convinced my dad to let me raise a few goats. I promised I would take full care of the goats, including milking them. I was to sell the milk to a man down the road who made cheese. I was allowed to keep the proceeds. Goats provide thick milk, which some of the neighbors really liked and were eager to buy. I personally did not like the stuff, so I never drank it. My mom made sure I saved every dime I made from the goats. I remember one time I held out on the goat money and bought my mother what I thought was the most beautiful hat. I knew when I saw the bonnet in the little shop in town, I had to buy it for my mom. Of course, she raised the dickens and protested that it was a terrible expense. But I told her how beautiful she looked and the whole family agreed. They thought she looked so good in the bonnet; she relented and kept it for special occasions.

As I got bigger Dad taught me how to plow with our big Percheron draft horse we called the General. He was an incredibly powerful horse and he pulled me down several times while plowing if I happened to hit a stump or big rock. We were self-sufficient with our own food and grew enough to bring a fair amount to sell on market days. On Saturdays we would hook up the General to the big flat wagon my dad had. Then we would load up all sorts of produce we grew on the farm and some cheese from the man down the road. Mom and my sister would churn butter on Fridays, and we would bring that along too. It must have been good butter because it always sold out. Dad and I did a lot of hunting. Deer, rabbits, and pheasants were a big part of our food supply. My dad was a crack shot, and I can't remember his ever missing. He taught me to shoot as well, and we had a wonderful time hunting. Then there was fishing too. There was a small lake not far from our farm, Dad and I would stroll down and catch a basket of fish which my mom always cooked for dinner that night.

Life was good on the farm, and I loved my family and had no thought of ever doing anything but farming. It was what we Sweeneys did. I enjoyed school and my pals. One of them was a fellow named Tom Edison. He didn't like school, and the teacher used to tease him all the time. I liked Tom and I thought he was a lot smarter than me. He was always fooling with some electrical gadget. He dropped out of school, and he told me his mom was going to be his teacher. Tom was a little hard of hearing, which people mistook for a bad attitude or dumbness.

Our teacher in that single-room schoolhouse thought Tom was not too bright. Reverend G. B. Engle, our teacher, sometimes called him names that implied Tom was stupid. I knew Tom and I can tell you he was the smartest kid I ever knew. Tom and I had some fun together as boys discovering the world. We would swim in the lake. I taught Tom how to fish. While we were in school, we hung out together a lot. Tom liked to show me the things he was making. He had a little chemistry lab set up in the little shack behind his family's brick home.

Our house was made of wood; they called it a Queen Anne home, but I never knew why. It had three floors, and my room was on the top floor. I do know it had a wonderful front porch and Mom used to spend a lot of time out there sewing and chatting with neighbors. Dad made sure it was always sparkling white with a black roof. A white picket fence surrounded the house. From the back porch we could look out over the farm. Out front we had this black iron pipe with a horse head on it for hitching a horse when someone came to visit.

Tom told me that he used to live in Malin, Ohio. Here he had a brick home. We would go there to Tom's "lab" and Tom would mix anything he could find to see what would happen. Sometimes the concoction bubbled, sometimes it changed color and occasionally, it made a big bang, especially when he lit a candle under the jar.

I remember meeting and liking Tom's father Samuel Edison Jr., who sometimes entertained us with stories of his adventures in Ontario, Canada where he was part of what he said was the Mackenzie rebellion, for which he had to flee the country and come to America. His mom Nancy Eliot Edison was genuinely nice and adored Tom. She was a little odd and so unlike my mom. Tom said she was sad because she had lost two children in childbirth.

Tom got a job as a newsboy delivering newspapers to homes and businesses. He built an ingenious wagon to hold the stack of newspapers while at the same time making it easy for him to reach in and toss them to the door of the house at each address on his list. Tom had all sorts of gadgets he made. He loved to talk about one day visiting far-off places. He knew a lot more than I did about the world. One day he showed me a book of maps, an atlas. We pored through it together, talking about the far-off places like China we would one day like to visit. I think my friend Thomas Edison planted the idea in my head that one day I would like to go to the sea and see the world. I heard that Tom eventually moved when his dad took a job as a lighthouse keeper and carpenter on the Fort Gratiot Military Post near Port Huron, Michigan. When he was 12, Thomas Edison started selling candies and newspapers on the Grand Trunk Railroad, which carried passengers to and from Detroit. Not only did Edison set up a chemistry lab in the baggage car, but he also built a printing press for an original newspaper he created, *The Grand Trunk Herald*.

Another friend of mine and classmate was Ezekiel Henry. We called him Zeke. He was a big lad much like me and loved the outdoors as well. Zeke lived in town with his parents in a great big house. He had two sisters and a younger brother. His mom was genuinely nice and often gave us milk and cookies after school. His dad was a lawyer. I wasn't sure what that meant, but I did notice that his dad was dressed every day the way my dad dressed on Sundays. I asked Zeke what a lawyer did, and he explained that mainly he helped people when they got into trouble and were arrested. That seemed to me to be a good thing. My dad knew Zeke's father and said he was a right smart gentleman. Zeke liked the farm, especially the animals. The summer he would come over often and spend the day helping me and tending to the animals. Zeke Henry especially liked my goats. I think maybe he liked my sister too.

Then one day Dad hitched up the surrey and took me on a trip with him to the city of Sandusky in Ohio. Dad had some business to do and told me I could roam around the city but to not wander off from the port area. Dad never told me what other business he had but I know he wore a suit and had a lot of paper in his satchel. My brother John told me one day he thought Dad dabbled in real estate.

On another trip my father took me again to Sandusky, Ohio. Dad dropped me off near a used book shop. There were more books there than I had ever seen. When an old gentleman asked what book, I was looking for, I said I didn't know which book, but I wanted to know all about those tall sailing ships out there at the docks. He said he knew just the book for me. In a few minutes, the old gentleman hobbled back with a well-worn book.

When I asked how much, the gentleman said, "A quarter."

I guess he recognized the look on my face. I did not have a quarter to spend. Then he said, for you today it would be ten cents. I eagerly fished for the dime I had, which I was saving for an ice cream. I took the dime out of my pocket and bought the book. Then we headed out again to see the tall ships. When I met my dad, he was surprised to see me carrying a book. On the way home he chatted about ships and told me about his dad who was a seafaring man back in Ireland. I had not known that and was thrilled to hear the sea stories about Grandfather.

Dad was born in Ohio, and he had never been to sea. The same was true of my mother, but she had some tales her parents told her about the tough times they had sailing over from Ireland before she was born. As time went on, I read the book over and over again. I devoured every page, almost seeing myself actually doing the things the author described in the book. By the age of fourteen, wanderlust had me in its grip. I had saved up twenty-five dollars, and as painful as it was to leave my family, I made the decision to seek my fortune at sea. Mom was in tears when I broke the news of my intentions. Dad said it was time for the lad to make his way in life and he gave me his blessing. He gave me his pocketknife which he had gotten from his dad. There was a lot of teasing from my brothers. and sisters until I left a few weeks later. Mom gave me a sack of cornbread and apples. I gave the goats to my younger brother. Then I headed off to seek my fortune at sea.

D AD TOOK ME in the buggy to Port Huron. He knew a man at the Palmer and Miller Feed store who got me a ride with a delivery man who was heading back to Sandusky. As we rode along, the driver, a man named Rusty and I talked about my plan to get to New York City and my dream to go to sea. He was extremely interested and told me that he thought the riverboat out of Sandusky could get me to Buffalo, New York. Rusty said he had sometimes picked up freight from the boat. They were bringing in all sorts of stuff, like wine, furniture, and farm machinery. Also, they were bringing lots of people, some from Ireland and some from Germany. He said it got so you couldn't understand a word of what they were saying.

When we arrived at Sandusky on Lake Erie, Rusty brought the wagon to a warehouse right near the steamboat dock. I helped him unhitch the horses and hang the tack. When that was done, he invited me to his home for dinner. He said I looked like I could use a bath and a place to sleep. After a bath, I went to dinner. Dinner was wonderful. I really had not had a home-cooked meal like that since I left home. Rusty's wife Mary was a warm and sweet person, and I liked her very much. She had two boys, about ages six and seven. They were lively kids and wanted to hear all about where I came from. After dinner, we stayed on the porch for a while and Mary asked if I would like to join the family for Sunday mass. I remembered I had promised my mother that I would get to mass every Sunday and receive communion. I said I would be happy to join them, which I did. After mass, Rusty took us all for a look at the steamboat docks. He thought I might be able to earn some money helping passengers get from their carriages to and from the docks. He was right.

The next day I watched as some boys my age helped and received tips from the well-dressed passengers. Rusty left me at the docks and said if I needed a place to sleep, I could bunk in his hayloft anytime. I thanked him and said I would be glad to, and I would feed the horses and muck out his barn in the morning. I found an out-of-the-way spot on the docks where I could learn what was going on and how I could go about helping passengers and earning tip money. The next day when I got through mucking out and straightening up Rusty's barn, I walked over to the docks. It was not long before I heard a steamboat whistle. The steamboat *War Eagle* was arriving from Buffalo. There were boys and some men at the gangplank eager to do what I hoped to do. A few gave me a threatening stare, not very happy about the competition. But there were plenty of passengers with plenty of luggage and steam trunks. The next

4

morning, I was back on the docks hoping to catch arriving passengers and help them with their luggage. I was hoping to accumulate enough tip money to pay for a ticket on the steamboat *War Eagle*.

The first thing I saw coming into Buffalo Harbor was the elongated shape and cream color of the Buffalo Harbor Lighthouse at the entrance to the harbor. The friendly captain allowed me to stand next to the helmsman. He saw me staring at the wheelhouse and he sensed how eager I was to learn the way of ships. He told me that he had been the captain of a sailing vessel many years before. The captain knew a great deal about the lighthouse. He said it had a four-panel Fresnel lens turned "on a combination mercury pot and ball bearing support," producing a white flash every five seconds. The light, whose source was an oil vapor lamp, had a strength of 180,000 candlepower and a range of 15 ¾ miles. I asked him why the light flashed and did not just stay on. He explained the way to identify which lighthouse or navigation marker in the dark was by the duration of the flash. He said the exact time of the flash of each light is listed on the charts. That made a lot of sense. The captain offered me a job for the summer, and I accepted. My job was to help out wherever needed. A kind of jack of all trades. One day I might be loading freight, the next painting or splicing a line. The engineer taught me how to oil the bearings for the big paddle wheel. One of the crewmen taught me how to make a splice in a line and how to make a bowline knot. Whenever I had some free time, I would bring a cup of hot coffee to the helmsman and try to talk him into allowing me to steer when we were in open water with no risk of my running the boat aground. From time to time, I would run into Rusty at the dock in Sandusky. At the end of that summer, I headed for the Erie Canal

The captain of the steamboat *War Eagle* had shown me the route I would have to take to get to New York. It involved my following the Erie Canal route and, if I got lucky, getting a ride on a canal boat to the city of Troy, New York then down the Hudson River to Manhattan. To find the way to the Erie Canal I first had to get to the canal at Lockport. Once again, I was fortunate enough to hitch a ride with a teamster bringing freight from the Steamboat *War Eagle* to Lockport for shipment in a canal boat. The teamster was very helpful. He spoke to one of the horse drivers he knew and told him I had a lot of experience working with horses. That conversation convinced the driver that I could be a big help. The canal boats were towed along the canal by a team of horses or mules that walked on a towpath next to the canal. The men that drove the horses were called "hoggees." The boats were called "packet boats" and were usually between 60 and 80 feet long and roughly 14 feet wide. The capacity was 60 passengers. When we reached the first bridge we shouted "bridge" which was a warning to the passengers on deck that they needed to duck down. The bridges were very low; they just cleared the roof of the canal boat. The canal was forty feet wide and about 4 feet deep. I observed that when two canal boats passed each other, there wasn't much room between the shore and each other and between their midships. The boat crews used poles to maintain as little distance as possible between two boats. There were 83 locks from one end of the canal to the other. I had never seen a lock before and wondered how it worked.

I soon learned at the first lock, that Lake Erie was 583 feet higher than the Hudson River. That meant a boat going from Lake Erie to the Hudson River would have to be lowered down 583 feet over a distance of 400 miles. I was amazed that the canal cut through fields, forests, and rocky cliffs. I wondered how in the world they did it. Who was it that came up with the idea? I learned that states like Michigan and Ohio were rich in timber, minerals, and fertile land for farming. It took weeks to reach these precious resources. Travelers were faced with a rough ride on over-rutted turnpike roads that baked to hardness in the summer sun. In the winter, the roads dissolved into a sea of mud. Wheels sank down, horses were often injured, and mules simply sat down and refused to move. It was a terrible mess.

Thomas Jefferson once investigated the idea of building a canal. But it was not until the idea was resurrected by a man who had personal knowledge of the problem, one Jesse Hawley. A flour merchant, Hawley envisioned a better way while serving time in prison. He had gone bankrupt trying to get his product to market from what is now Rochester. Sent to debtor's prison as a result, Hawley wrote a series of essays which were published in the Genesee Messenger newspaper beginning in 1807, describing in great detail the route, costs, and benefits of what would become the Erie Canal. He envisioned a canal from Buffalo on the eastern shore of Lake Erie to Albany on the upper Hudson River. After years of political maneuvering and some failed attempts at building a canal, New York's Governor DeWitt Clinton got behind the project and pushed it through. Eventually he became Canal Commissioner.

He argued, *"The city will, in the course of time, become the granary of the world, the emporium of commerce, the seat of manufactures, the focus of great moneyed operations,"* said Clinton. *"And before the revolution of a century, the whole island of Manhattan, covered with inhabitants and replenished with a dense population, will constitute one vast city."*

At first, the canal commission tried to hire European engineers experienced in building canals to engineer the canal. They weren't interested. So American engineers were hired and broke ground on the Erie Canal on July 4, 1817, just outside Rome, New York. Work commenced with the 90-mile middle section of the canal where there were the fewest natural impediments like rocky cliffs or swamps. Construction got off to a good start, so Clinton contracted out the work to local landowners, who were responsible for hiring the laborers to dig the canal. They were paid from 50 cents to a dollar a day. Imagine how hard it was to dig the dirt out with a shovel. I know I hated digging out ditches back on my dad's farm. My boss told me that from 1818 to 1819, around three thousand men and 700 horses labored every day to dig the section of the Erie Canal from Utica to the Seneca River. He said it was nasty work and he quit after the first day. The work slowed when they encountered a soggy and mosquito-plagued region called the Montezuma swamps. The local farmers refused to work in the terrible conditions where what they called "Genesee fever" was killing laborers at an alarming rate. The contractors turned to Irish immigrants who had arrived in New York Harbor. Thousands of Irish laborers were sickened or died in the swamps, yet they continued to work and eventually took over the work from local laborers. That caused a drastic increase in anti-Irish, anti-Catholic sentiment The Irish workers were often paid in whiskey in addition to (or sometimes in place of) their meager wages of $12 a month. While brawling and skirmishes with locals were a frequent problem, the Irish workers proved willing to do the dirtiest and most dangerous work, including blasting rock with unpredictable black powder. At long last, the canal opened in 1825.

I did a lot of walking as a hoggee, driving the horses that towed the canal boat. It must have been nearly 400 miles from Buffalo to Troy. After he was sure I could handle the horses by myself, my boss started riding in the canal boat. I would hold the horses as the canal boat would be raised or lowered in the lock. I never really got to ride in a Canal boat, but I did watch it go through the locks a total of 83 times. I never got bored watching the boat go into the lock while the gate ahead was closed. Then two or three men closed the gates behind the boat. The gates were constructed so that the high water on one side would hold them firmly in place. The lock attendant would open some valves and the water level in the lock would lower, taking the canal boat with it. That done, the men would walk to the other end of the lock and open the other gate. Then I would tow the boat out of the lock on down the canal. At long last we arrived at West Troy, New York.

3

Next, I had to figure out the way to get down the Hudson River to New York City. It turned out to be much easier than I thought. I just followed the passengers disembarking from the canal boat. The majority, I learned, were also heading for New York City. Some were taking the railroad and some, like me, were taking a steamboat. There were actually eight different boats running from Albany to New York. I had not expected to be paid for my work as a hoggee, so when my boss handed me some money, I was truly delighted to get it. I used the money to buy a ticket on the steamboat *SS George Washington.* For the first time in my life, I was a paying passenger, I enjoyed every minute of it. The trip down the Hudson River was magnificent. The *SS George Washington* was beautiful, and the interior was, as one passenger described it, "A floating palace." She was 225 feet in length and displaced 700 tons. I even splurged for lunch in the restaurant onboard. The restaurant offered some great sandwiches and free oysters. I tried an oyster and ate the chicken sandwich. One of the passengers, a lovely young girl not much older than me, who saw me trying to discreetly ditch the oyster, told me it was an acquired taste and that one day I would eat a dozen and love them. We reached New York City by nightfall. I just walked through Manhattan from the steamboat dock heading south and drinking up the amazing sights of a big city.

From my reading I knew that if I wanted to find a ship sailing to China, I would have to get myself to South Street. In what seemed like years, but was actually more like months, I finally made it to New York City and the waterfront. I still had nearly $25.00 hidden in my pants.

The aroma of the waterfront around South Street filled my nostrils. It was a combination of salt air, tar, fish, wood, paint, and canvas all rolled into one wonderful contrast to the smell of hay, wheat, and cow manure.

I wandered around the docks for several days. At night I would find a coil of rope or on bales of hay to sleep on. Then one day I asked an old sailor how I could get a job on a ship. He pointed me to a storefront building that was the place where sailors went to find a berth on ship. The old fellow told me they would never hire me as an able-bodied seaman, but I might get a berth as a cabin boy. It was a noisy place with lots of salty looking men hanging around telling sea stories to each other and spitting into brass bowls on the floor. Every so often a man would stand at the front of the room and announce the name of a ship looking for a crew. I watched this procedure for a few days. Then when the sailing vessel *Victory* bound for Peking was announced, I got on the line. At the desk I asked if there was a berth for a cabin boy. It was a dusty old building with a bunch of benches and a big chalkboard up front. The chalkboard had listed those ships that were sailing and what crews they needed. The man looked over a sheet of paper and said, "As a matter of fact, young laddy, there is." He said make your mark here and head out to the ship which was tied up right there in front street. She was a four-masted Schooner named *Victory*. When I asked the man what it meant to "make your mark," he said, "Sign your name." He was quite surprised and laughed out loud when he learned I could read and write.

I WAS DELIRIOUS WITH excitement. At last, I was going to sea and maybe going to China. I was pretty big for my age, so lying that I was sixteen instead of fourteen was an easy trick. The mate that stood at the top of the gangplank didn't seem to care. He checked my name off his list and directed me to the back part of the ship which I soon learned was called aft. Another fellow my age introduced himself as Sean Kelly. He said he had just signed on but had already done a voyage as a cabin boy. Both of us being Irish, we seemed to hit it off right away. Sean showed me where I would bunk and then told me I should report to Mr. Larsen who was the first mate. Crewmen were coming aboard as I approached Mr. Larsen on what I learned was the quarter-deck. He was a gruff kind of man of few words.

He asked, "Are you the other cabin boy?"

"Yes sir."

"Stand over there."

I had read stories of how brutal a ship's officer could be and stood there dreading Mr. Larsen's next move.

After about a half hour Mr. Larsen said "OK, my fair young laddies, let's go meet the captain."

We walked aft to the captain's cabin which was much more ornate than I would have ever imagined.

Mr. Larsen knocked, and I heard a voice, "Come in."

Captain Christopher Livingston was a big man with a handsome face, square-jawed and a thick head of golden blond hair. He had a neatly trimmed beard. He seemed friendly enough, not nearly as scary as I had imagined he would be.

The captain said, "So son, you want to be a cabin boy."

I stood straight and answered, "Yes, sir."

The captain said, "You will be my assistant. You will fetch my meals, run errands, clean my cabin, make my bed, empty my chamber pot and do anything I need you to do. And when the weather gets bad, you will lend a hand with the lines, help with pumps, and generally try to keep yourself from being washed overboard or hit with anything that might be flying around on deck. You will be at my beck and call twenty-four hours a day, seven days a week. And when I need you to climb to the top of the main mast, you will do so.

"Is that OK with you lad?"

"Yes, sir."

"Sweeney, you are dismissed."

My dream of going to sea was about to begin. Curled up in my canvas bunk that night, I could not sleep a wink. Early the next morning I arose at dawn to see lots of activity on deck. Sean soon joined me and said we were getting ready to sail on the morning tide.

As we slowly moved out of the harbor, I realized that for the first time in my life, I was on a ship heading downriver and out into the vast ocean.

The captain shouted, "Sweeney!" and I ran to the quarter deck.

He said, "Get me and Mr. Larsen some coffee here, and make damn sure it is hot."

"Yes, sir," I said, and slid down the quarter deck ladder. Luckily, Sean was at the foot of the ladder. I whispered, "Where do I get the coffee?"

Sean said, "Follow me."

We ran along the deck to a hatch and down the steep stairway. Sean introduced me to a big light brown skinned man he called Cookie. Cookie had a lot of tattoos on his arms and even on his neck. I tried not to stare, but Cookie noticed. He smiled a great big grin and pointed to his tattoo of a naked woman.

Cookie said, "That be my Matilda. She sleep with me every night and never give me no heartache."

Cookie gave me two mugs of coffee. Luckily, he pressed some wooden lids on the mugs to keep them from spilling.

I ran back to the quarter deck with the hot coffee and gave it to the Captain and Mr. Larsen. Mr. Larsen then told me to go find Sean and have him show me how to clean up the captain's quarters. I found Sean chewing on a biscuit and watching the shore as we moved down river and out through the Narrows. I asked if that was breakfast? Sean said, you missed breakfast, but you might get Cookie to give you one of these. I heard some other men call him "Doc." I told Sean what Mr. Larsen had said and Sean said sure, He then broke his biscuit in half and gave me half. Sean said we wouldn't have time to see Cookie right now and would have to get right to work in the captain's quarters. I chewed the biscuit on the way. It didn't have any taste and was dry but, I was so hungry it didn't matter.

Sean showed me where to dump out the chamber pot and make up the captain's bunk. Then he took me into the captain's office quarters. I was amazed at how big it was and at all the books it contained. It had lots of brass things I did not recognize. Sean showed me how to straighten up the desk, sweep the floor, and make the place neat.

As we worked, I asked about Cookie. Sean said Cookie was from some South Sea Island and had been a chef there. Sean said some of the scuttlebutt he heard claimed Cookie came from a cannibal tribe, but Sean said others told him that was not true. Sean warned me not to believe everything the seamen told me. By the time we finished overhauling the captain's quarters, it was noon, and the sun was shining brightly, lighting up the sails like great walls of light. The air was fresh, and the wind was blowing crisp and clean.

That half of a biscuit wasn't nearly enough. A far cry from the eggs, sausage, and biscuits my mom made every morning back on the farm. My stomach was aching for some food.

Just then, Sean came by and said, "Hey Sweeney, let's get some grub before it's all gone."

Cookie had made a meat stew with lots of vegetables and bread; it was really good, and I wondered why some of the sailors griped about it.

Cookie said, "Don't you worry dem boys like to be moanin' 'bout my cookin'." Watch dem eat down, den you know they be likin' it fine. Now you bring dis tray to de captain and be quick about it."

I knocked on the captain's door.

He said 'Come in. Aw Sweeney, I was getting hungry, and you arrived at just the right time." He asked, "Tell me, son, what made you want to go to sea?"

I told the captain about the book I had bought and how it sounded like an exciting thing to do. I noticed the captain's grub was much better than what we got. It consisted of a nice piece of steak and some boiled vegetables all covered with gravy. I supposed that is only right since he was the captain. But I sure wished I had a meal like that. I could not help but notice the thick gravy clinging to the captain's beard. He had a handlebar mustache.

The captain asked me if I liked to read.

I said, "Yes sir, reading is my favorite thing."

He said, "Well then, I will loan you a book or two as we go to help you know the ways of the sea. Take care of them. Books are very special to me, and I don't truck with them being mishandled."

The captain then chose a book from the shelf and handed it to me. The cover was worn, and the pages frayed at the edges. It was a small book about a boy about my age who went to sea as a cabin boy. That night I started reading the book by the light from the brass oil lamp I had hung over my bunk. I was getting used to the aroma emanating into my humble quarters in the bilge.

I was fascinated by the cabin boy's adventures and soon I began to identify with the boy in the book while at the same time learning what my job would be. As the weeks turned into months, I began to feel as if I was a part of the ship's crew.

5

*V*ICTORY WAS WHAT is known as a three-masted brig. I didn't know it at the time, but she was one of the fastest sailing vessels on the seas. And she was truly beautiful, with the sails billowing in the wind. I can't think of anything I have ever seen that is more beautiful.

There was a lot of activity on the decks as cargo was loaded into the holds. Barrels, a large cask called a hogshead, boxes, and all sorts of stuff were put aboard. Even some live pigs, chickens, and a few cows. There was shooting, cursing, and creaking of pulleys. I was warned to stay clear of the booms. It was exciting to see all the activity and then finally to see the crew put boards on the hatches and cover them with canvas to make them watertight.

A half dozen seamen put one of our longboats over the side and then started rowing toward the bow of our ship. Then another seaman threw them a line he had attached to the ship. I was amazed to see that a small boat with only six men rowing could move a big ship like the *Victory*. Slowly the ship moved clear of the dock.

Then I heard Mr. Larsen shout, "Hoist the main!"

Seamen seemed to be coming out of nowhere. Several started climbing up the rigging and out onto the yards. In what seemed like minutes the great white sails unfurled and blossomed out. I could feel the ship start to move. By that time the longboat had come aside, and the men were climbing up the side. In no time they had the longboat back aboard and in place.

Mr. Larsen was shouting commands like "Up the main sail! Up the top sail!"

I watched in amazement as sailors hauled lines that had been hung neatly on the side of the deck. Suddenly they were causing sails to rise above me. I heard several loud bangs as the wind caught the sails. We were underway.

As we slowly moved out of New York harbor I realized that for the first time in my life, I was on a ship heading down river and out into the vast ocean. My dreams were becoming reality. It was beautiful. *Victory* was a beautiful ship. I was told that a man named John Griffiths had designed the ship and that it was built at the Smith and Dimons New York shipyard. She was 280 feet long and 36 feet wide, and she drew 21 feet. She carried a crew of 28 to 30 souls, with 32,000 square feet of sail. There were about 50 sails. Her gross tonnage was 963 net 621.

The excitement of setting sail with all the activity involved soon faded but will live in my memory forever. Things got pretty routine once we cleared the harbor and were in open water. I watched for a while as the land seemed to grow smaller and smaller, then disappear into the horizon. Occasionally a massive fish would jump out of the water and follow the boat for a time. Sean told me they were porpoises. I was happy to know they were porpoises because I had heard some nasty things about sharks. At one point we spotted a ship Sean said was a whaler from New England. He told me that these ships were out of New Bedford, Massachusetts in search of whales. I had read a little about whales back in school in Celina.

He said the ships might stay out at sea for three or four years or until their holds were filled with whale oil. Sean said that a whaler could make a lot of money if the catch was good. Mostly the whalers came out of New England and Nantucket where there were many stories of whales attacking ships. One famous case was the whale ship *Essex*, attacked and sunk by an angry whale. Starving in their long boats, the crew eventually turned to cannibalism. The whaler we passed must have recently landed a whale because there was a lot of activity on deck and smoke coming from midship where the crew was boiling down blubber to store as whale oil. A very strong odor from the ship wafted over us.

OUR FIRST BIG storm was something I will never forget. The sky started out clear and bright that morning, then slowly turned to gray as the temperature dropped. The wind picked and the ship gained more speed. But then the sea got rough, and the ship began to pound through enormous waves. The captain ordered the sails reduced and the ship secured for heavy weather. Lines were strung across the deck to keep crew members from being washed overboard. Torrents of sea water blasted across the deck as the bow dipped into the waves. All the crew members on deck donned their oil cloths and sou'wester hats. Everything that could move was lashed down, the hatches and the longboats secured. The sky grew black as the ship rose to the top of each wave, then fell off. There were times when the ship leaned over to a point where the sails nearly touched the sea, then miraculously came back up only to lean again. The pounding and rolling went on all night. By dawn the storm subsided, and the sun broke through the dark clouds. The sea grew calm, and the giant waves turned into gentle rollers. Everything was wet. When I crawled into my bunk, exhausted, yet tingling with the thrill of my first storm, the damp went right through my clothes.

When I talked with Sean about the storm, he said he was scared, and I had to admit I was too. Mr. Larsen said that we should not worry too much about it. He said *Victory* was a well-built ship and could take a beating.

A good portion of our cargo was ginseng, a wild root that grew in the Hudson Valley. I had never heard of ginseng, but Mr. Larsen told me the Chinese loved it and used a lot of it. He said one of the first cargos brought to China from the USA was ginseng. On their return voyage, the Americans carried home tea, fireworks, porcelain, silks, and sometimes opium. There was an extremely big demand for tea from China in England. A 500 British pound bonus and the highest prices were paid to the first captain who brought the new crop.

We headed south to round Cape Horn. Mostly the seas were calm, and the sun was warm, but at one point it started getting cold and ice formed on the sails. The mate said we would have to find warmer weather to melt the ice which endangered the ship. We sailed a few hundred miles off course to find the warmth we needed to defrost the sails.

By the time we reached Cape Horn, the weather was getting colder and the sea growing rougher. The crew was frantically trying just about everything to keep from being blown overboard. I had heard stories of how the "Horn" could be bad but so far things were not as bad as I imagined. Then it hit, waves like mountains, freezing rain, and hailstones that hit your face like buckshot. The ratlines whistled in the wind, the sails looked as if they were about to burst, and the ship creaked under the strain. The captain ordered the mainsails trimmed. We used just the topsails. One old seaman called the waves "graybeards", He recalled the line "The graybeards had made a mockery of his oil skin. "The lookout endured the salty blast and ice bullets to watch for icebergs. Even with less sail, we were racing along at a rapid pace. Salt water soaked the deck and everyone on it. Lifelines were run because it was impossible to walk across the pitching deck without risking being washed overboard. Crewmen took turns manning the pumps. I volunteered, but they told me I wasn't yet old enough to be able to work a bilge pump. The pounding and pitching went on for three days and nights. Then just as quickly as it had come upon us, the storm was over, and the skies cleared.

That night something really strange happened. I was on deck with Sean enjoying the moonlight and calm seas when suddenly an eerie blue light flashed across the yards and down along the masts to the deck. First Mate Larsen said it was St Elmo's fire. It only lasted a few minutes, but it was an incredible sight to see. It scared me and Sean for a moment but then we enjoyed seeing it.

Mr. Larsen told me that we would be putting into port at Valparaiso. I had never heard of it, so I was eager to find out all about it. I thought it would be nice to walk around on land a little after so many days at sea. I asked the captain if he had a book about Valparaiso, and he said he did. Valparaiso is in Chile. After we rounded the cape, we had to sail north to reach it. We needed to take on water and lots of fresh vegetables, fruits, and meat. Mr. Larsen had advised me to eat as many oranges and lemons as we could find to prevent scurvy. Some of sailors said it was a good place to get some rum and some women. I had a taste of rum a few weeks out and frankly, I did not like it, and particularly did not like the funny way it made me feel.

W<small>E DROPPED ANCHOR</small> in the bay at Valparaiso. The Captain went ashore to arrange for provisions and to see if he could get passengers who might be going to San Francisco, our next port. In a few hours several small boats came out to the ship. They had casks of water, hogsheads of wine, and several large wooden boxes. The crew took them aboard and lowered them into the hold using a kind of crane they fashioned utilizing the main mast and a sail boom. With that done, some of the crew were allowed to go ashore. Things were pretty quiet on the ship until after dark when some of the crew returned. They seemed incredibly happy except for a fellow named Hans Norden. Hans was a really big strong guy. I had seen him lift some heavy crates by himself. Generally speaking, Hans had always been genuinely nice to me. But that night he was very drunk and very angry with anyone he encountered. He swung out at anyone who tried to talk to him. Then he punched one of the crewmen who tried to help him walk. He was staggering and falling over the hatches. Mr. Larsen heard the commotion and came up on deck. He ordered Hans to go below, but Hans was in a fighting mood. He swung at Mr. Larsen, Mr. Larsen ducked just in time and Hans fell to the deck. As he tried to get up Mr. Larsen hit him over the head with a belaying pin. On a sailing ship a belaying pin is a solid metal or wooden device used on traditionally rigged sailing vessels to secure lines of the rigging They are very much like the nightstick's policeman carry.

That was the first time I had seen Mr. Larsen angry, and I was surprised that he was able to subdue Hans. Hans was bleeding and unconscious. Larsen called Hans a "son of a gun." The other crewmen carried Hans down to his bunk and things were calm for the rest of the night. The next morning the captain returned, and Mr. Larsen asked me if I wanted to join him on a visit ashore. While we were going ashore in the longboat, I asked Mr. Larsen what he meant when he called Hans a son of a gun.

He explained that it was an old Royal Navy expression that implied the person's mother was a woman of easy virtue and that person was conceived under a cannon on a Royal Navy Ship while it was in port. In short, it was like calling someone a bastard.

Larsen said he had things to do, but he would meet me for dinner later at eight bells right there on the pier where he left. He warned me to be careful and not to stray out of the city.

Valparaiso was an exciting town for a fellow like me who came from a farm. I headed for the center of the town. I could not believe what I saw there. The Church of the Savior is beautiful, bigger than anything I have ever seen. It had its origins in a series of religious groups dating back to about 1529. As I entered the church I was drawn to the altar. It was an altar like I had never seen before. It was decorated with lots and lots of gold. The top of it nearly touched the ceiling. There were statues everywhere. It was so quiet, I felt like I should only whisper. And there was the aroma of incense like when the priest back in Celina lighted the thurible, which always makes me feel religious. I spent a long time looking at the church. Then after a while an old priest came out. He said he was a Jesuit and he asked me where I was from. The priest was very nice and spoke English with a Spanish accent. He invited me to lunch, which was great. Lunch consisted of black olives, cheese, the most wonderful bread I have ever tasted, and small pieces of chicken in a tomato sauce. He also gave me a small glass of wine, a burgundy made from grapes grown in the church's vineyard. The priest wanted to know all about where I came from and where I was going. He asked if I was Catholic and after lunch gave me communion. The priest told me about the church which he said had been robbed and burned several times. As I said goodbye, he gave me a small wooden crucifix with a leather band to wear around my neck. As I left, he gave me a blessing.

I spent the afternoon walking all around Valparaiso. My head was a little fuzzy, but I felt happy. It is a beautiful city with lots of houses painted bright colors and a lovely town square. There were some wonderful shops with all kinds of things I would have liked to buy for my mother and sister. But I did not buy anything. I was saving my money for San Francisco.

8

⚓

WE WEIGHED ANCHOR early in the morning and set sail for San Francisco. I got to talk to the dozen passengers we had aboard. They were all heading to California to dig for gold. Some of them were old and had been digging for gold in places all over the country. Some were younger with no experience, just the desire to strike it rich. The weather was good, with a fine breeze. Perfect weather for sailing. We made it to San Francisco in record time. From a pilot boat waiting for us, a pilot came aboard and guided the ship into the harbor and to a pier in what is called the Embarcadero section. The passengers all disembarked, and the crew was given some time to enjoy the town.

Some of our cargo was offloaded, and we put on some more. The crew was excited about getting into the city. Those kept on watch were a little annoyed. They would get their turn. Luckily Sean and I were allowed to leave the ship early in the morning. We just about ran to the area where there were stores. It was incredible. Every store window seemed to have better and brighter things. I had been told that I could get some nice things for my mom in Chinatown. I spotted some beautiful scarves that were not too expensive but beautiful. One of them had this giant peacock with its feathers all fanned out. The other was a beautiful garden scene. I bought one for my mom and one for my sister. Each cost one dollar. They had so many beautiful things, they had my head spinning. Sean bought a few scarves too.

Sean spotted a Chinese restaurant with a giant dragon out front. He said he had never tasted Chinese food and wanted to go in for a meal. That sounded like a good idea to me, so in we went, The place smelled of incense and had a lot of colorful lanterns on the walls. There were lots and lots of decorations related to China. In the center of the dining room, there was an enormous fish tank filled with the biggest goldfish I had ever seen. The tank was really swarming with fish, some of which we later learned you could order and have cooked for your meal. When we sat down at the table the waitress, a very attractive young Chinese girl in a silk dress with a high collar, brought us a menu. She spoke fairly good English so we asked her what she thought we should order. Her name, she said, was Mayling. She suggested we have a bowl of egg drop soup and for the main course, we have chicken chow mein. We agreed and in no time, Mayling was back with two bowls of soup made from the fin of a shark. Sean commented on the soup spoons which were made of porcelain. They worked very well, and we enjoyed the soup. When the chicken chow mein came, it was steaming hot and looked delicious. The thing was we could not find any forks, just chopsticks. Mayling showed us how to use the chopsticks. It took a little while and a few spills before Sean and I got the hang of it. She also suggested we might want to put some soy sauce on the chow mein. For dessert Mailing brought out some sliced oranges. Sean and I split the bill and gave Mayling a nice tip. It was a delightful experience. I think Sean now has a kind of crush on Mayling even though he only met her one time.

Mayling said it was OK, so Sean took the chopsticks with him as a souvenir. The rest of the afternoon we strolled through the Embarcadero and all its amazing sights. We did a lot of people-watching too. There were people from all over, China, Spain, Europe, Ireland, and America, and of course us.

I noticed a Chinese guy at the next table who had soup with what looked like a bird's nest in the middle of the bowl. I quietly asked Mayling what that was the man was eating and she confirmed that it was a bird's nest. She said, "Vellie good."

We stayed in San Francisco for three days; then Mr. Larsen said we would sail on the early morning tide. Our next stop would be Honolulu. Honolulu is on the island of Hawaii, way out there in the ocean off San Francisco. The small boats were in the water just after dawn. The crew started rowing to tow the shop out to where she could raise the sails. That took a little more than an hour, but soon the crews rowed the boats back and hauled them. We had a pilot on board this time too. Mr. Larsen knew the pilot and they had an enjoyable time talking as he guided the ship out of the harbor and into the open sea. I really liked San Francisco. One day I would like to visit there again.

The air was crisp and clear, and we hoisted more sail and headed for Hawaii. My job as a cabin boy included a lot of time in the galley working with the cook. I had to bring provisions to the cook for the Lazarette. Often, I had to stick my hands into a barrel and bring out the salt pork that was stored in salty brine. It was my job to bring meals to the captain in his cabin and to set the table for the meal when he directed the cook that he was taking his meals in his cabin. Most of the time the captain took his meals with the other officers. Sean and I would bring meals to the officers' mess. We also carried the meals to the crew in the mess. We were also messenger boys. We carried messages back and forth between officers and the rest of the crew who occupied different parts of the ship. We had heard that we might be needed to go aloft to stow sails with the crew, and when the weather was good, we might stand a watch at the helm and learn how to steer the ship. So far, we had not been ordered to go aloft but it sounds like it could be great fun. I have had the opportunity to steer the ship several times now.

Another one of the jobs I got to do was when we were weighing anchor. As the crew members sang old chanty songs, they pushed hard on the capstan bars to raise the anchor. I had learned in one of my books that a capstan is a broad revolving cylinder with a vertical axis used for winding a rope or cable, pushed around by levers. My job was to keep flushing salt water on the anchor line, so it was clean of seaweed and jellyfish. When the anchor finally came up, it was my job to flush any sand that remained on it.

Mr. Larsen said I was on a merchant ship. He told me that on navy ships there were boys my age that worked as what they called Powder Monkeys. We did not have big naval cannons on *Victory* so there were no Powder Monkeys on *Victory*.

The seas were relatively calm on our trip to Hawaii, the skies were clear, and the wind was steady, which meant we did not have to alter sails for most of the trip.

9

I T WAS A much shorter trip from San Francisco to Hawaii than it had been from Valparaiso to San Francisco. It was on this leg of the trip that the captain first introduced me to the sextant. It was late afternoon and I had just brought a jug of hot coffee to the captain. He was on the bridge with Mr. Larsen. He held a shiny brass device in his hand and would hold it up to his eye from time to time. I waited until he asked for some coffee, then he asked if I knew what it was that he was holding in his hand. I said I did not, but I would like to know. As the captain sipped his coffee, he said that I should learn how to use the sextant. The captain said the sextant is a doubly reflecting navigation instrument that measures the angular distance between two visible objects. Use it to measure the angle between a star, the moon, or some other object in the sky and the horizon, and we can figure out where we are. I guess I must have looked a little bewildered. Then he said, "Never mind boy, I have a book in my cabin you can borrow to learn about the sextant."

Later that night the captain sent for me. Once I was in his cabin, he asked me to go over to the chart table and get the sextant out of the wooden box he kept it in. He showed me how to hold it up to my eye and look for the horizon. Then he took an old book off his desk and handed it to me. He told me to read it carefully and try to understand its purpose. That night after I finished my chores in the galley I climbed into my bunk and started to read the book. It was a little difficult reading because some of the words were new to me. Just as the captain had said that the sextant is used to measure angles, it said the estimation of this angle, the altitude, is known as sighting or shooting the object, or taking a sight." The angle, and the time when it was measured, can be used to calculate a position line on a nautical chart—for example, sighting the sun at noon or Polaris at night (in the Northern Hemisphere) to estimate latitude. Sighting the height of a landmark can give a measure of distance off and, held horizontally, a sextant can measure angles between objects for a position on a chart. A sextant can also be used to measure the lunar distance between the moon and another celestial object (such as a star or planet) to determine Greenwich Mean Time and hence longitude. I had seen the word longitude on a chart in the captain's cabin. The book was hard to read, but I kept at it night after night and it all started to become more understandable. About a week later, when I was in the captain's cabin having brought him coffee, he asked if I had been reading the book. Then he questioned me, and I guess I got it right because he patted me on the back and said, "Good job, boy." Once again, he told me to get the sextant, then he explained it further. The next day at noon he called me to the poop deck where he showed me how to shoot the sun. By the time we reached Hawaii, the captain had me shooting the sun every day at noon. First, he would shoot the sun then he would hand the sextant to me and ask me the angles.

Hawaii was a beautiful place. We entered Honolulu harbor, and once again we had taken on a pilot. As soon as we got into the harbor and turned to port heading for a berth, large canoes full of natives started paddling alongside the ship. They were wearing colorful sheets of cloth, and on their heads, flower wreaths. Some were beating little drums. They seemed friendly; the pilot did not seem alarmed nor was the captain. I soon realized they were selling fruit, flowers, and lots of other island products. The boats were dugouts set up with a smaller dugout to keep balanced. As they got closer to the ship, they threw us leis, flower necklaces. Several of the crew members put them on. They had an odd-looking plant the pilot said was a pineapple. It did not look like any apple I had ever seen, but I was eager to try this new fruit. Mr. Larsen said it was delicious.

The pilot was genuinely nice and spent some time telling me about Honolulu. He said people from across Asia and Europe arrived to work in the fields, all traveling through Honolulu Harbor. He said pineapples were shipped to the States. Some very tall trees that I had never seen before--palm trees. The coconut palm gives off a large coconut that is very much sought after for the coconut milk and the white meat inside the coconut.

Soon the crew put longboats over the side and the pilot directed the ship into a berth. As we settled in and the ship was tied up, I noticed several ships like the whaler we had seen months ago.

10

ONE OF THE crew told me that he had been to Honolulu several times and that he had seen a lot of whalers and had talked with them in some of the bars he liked to visit. He described how they caught the whales, which I found fascinating. He said the main thing they were after was blubber which they boiled down into whale oil. Then they would not head home until the hold was filled with casks of oil. The whalemen had a harder life than regular sailors. Sometimes whales attacked ships, actually making them break up. Sometimes a whale attacks the dory. And sometimes after a whaler throws a harpoon into a whale, it starts to swim very fast. The whalemen called that a Nantucket sleigh ride. Sometimes the whale towed the dory so far away from the whaleship that they had an exceedingly difficult time getting back to it. Sometimes they never did and were lost. At times, the ship would spend days looking for the dories and, of course, the whale carcass. He said they would tow the dead whale to the side of the whaleship and begin cutting off the thick layer of blubber jut under the whale's skin. They would cut it into chunks and put them into a big pot of boiling whale oil on deck. The blubber melted into whale oil, then was poured into casks and stored in the hold. The whale meat tasted like steak and was used to feed the crew. Whalers were always looking for ambergris, a jelly-like orange-colored mass that is sometimes found floating in the area near whales or inside the whales. Called ambergris, it is unbelievably valuable. It is used in the making of fine perfume.

Honolulu is an enchanting place. It is very warm and sunny. And there are lots of people wearing a traditional kind of dress that looks like they are wearing a colorful bed sheet. Some of the women wear a skirt made of grass. I watched one afternoon when several beautiful native girls danced an amazingly fast and interesting dance, they call the hula. The girls gyrated to the beat of drums in ways I did not know were possible.

Great idea: Sean wanted to take a ride in a horse carriage and see the whole city. The first place we visited was the Iolani Palace, the home of the king of Hawaii. All the time we were amazed at all the colorful birds and lots and lots of flowers. Monkeys were screeching in the trees. We had never seen a monkey before and found them intriguing. Sean tried to catch one, but they were too quick for him. The next stop was the Kawaiaha's Church, in Honolulu on the Island of Oahu. The driver said a lot of people call it the Westminster Abbey of Hawaii and the Protestant Mother Church of Hawaii.

There were so many interesting sights in Honolulu that we were worn out from all the sightseeing. When we got back to the ship, we were told we would be setting sail in the morning. We had lots of work to do. Several of the crew members who had spent their time ashore chasing women and drinking came back staggering, laughing, and stinking of liquor. Mr. Larsen sent them all to their bunks without a word.

I ASKED MR. LARSEN what opium was. He told me that it was a kind of tobacco that made the smoker sleep a lot and go into a kind of semi-consciousness. It originally came from India and Turkey, but was very popular in China. Ironically, opium found its way into China from North America. He said it was dangerous stuff because once you started smoking it, it was hard to quit. He said that many a man lost everything because of opium. He said there were places called opium dens in New York where people would go and smoke themselves like zombies for days and even weeks. He warned Sean and me to stay away from it because it could ruin our lives. He told us a little about the opium wars. It seems the Chinese government wanted to stop the influx of opium into China. So many people had become addicted to it that it was damaging the economy and lives of the Chinese.

The captain heard Mr. Larsen telling us about opium and volunteered to lend me a book about it, which he lent me a few days later. I learned that opium is a narcotic drug that is obtained from the unripe seedpods of the opium poppy that is native to what is now the country of Turkey. It was first introduced to China by Turkish and Arab traders in the late 6th or early 7th century A.D. Taken orally to relieve tension and pain, the drug was used in limited quantities until the 17th century. At that point, the practice of smoking tobacco spread from North America to China, and opium smoking soon became popular throughout the country. Opium addiction increased, and opium importations grew rapidly during the first century of the Qing Dynasty (1644–1911/12). By 1729 it had become such a problem that the Yongzheng emperor who ruled 1722 to 1735 prohibited the sale and smoking of opium. That failed to hamper trade, and in 1796 the Jiaging emperor outlawed opium importation and cultivation. Despite such decrees, however, the opium trade continued to flourish.

Early in the 18th century, the Portuguese found that they could import opium from India and sell it in China at a considerable profit. By 1773 the British had discovered the trade, and that year they became the leading suppliers of the Chinese market. The British East India Company established a monopoly on opium cultivation in the Indian province of Bengal, where they developed a method of growing opium poppies cheaply and abundantly. Other Western countries also joined in the trade, including the United States, which dealt in Turkish as well as Indian opium.

Britain and other European countries undertook the opium trade because of their Chronic trade imbalance with China. There was tremendous demand in Europe for Chinese tea, silks, and porcelain pottery, but there was correspondingly little demand in China for Europe's manufactured goods and other trade items. Consequently, Europeans had to pay for Chinese products with gold or silver. The opium trade created a steady demand among Chinese addicts for opium imported from the West. The opium trade solved this chronic trade imbalance. Once the ship was fully loaded, we set sail for England. Mr. Larsen said we were headed for the Pool of London. I did not understand what that meant but we were pretty busy, so I did not get to ask him to explain for a few days. Then after we were settled into a routine and the seas were calm, I got the chance to ask Mr. Larsen to tell me about the "Pool of London." He took me to the captain's cabin and to the chart table to show me the route we were going to take to get from Canton to London. The sailing route from the China sea ports to London is across the China Sea, then the Indian Ocean, rounding the southern tip of Africa into the Atlantic, generally passing to the. west of the Azores, turning towards the English Channel and the Pool of London. We had a journey of roughly 14,000 miles ahead of us.

12

O N THIS LONG leg of our journey, I got to steer frequently during calm weather. The helmsman was always nearby, but there were times when I felt as if I was totally in charge of steering the ship, and I loved it. Increasingly, I became comfortable with keeping a close eye on the compass. At first, it was difficult to keep steady but after a while, I learned that I was steering too much. There were several days when there was so little wind the sails just flapped. Steering in that kind of calm is very boring. We had very good weather on most of the trip and before long we were in the English Channel. Once again, we took on a pilot and headed for a place that was almost as busy and crowded as Canton Harbor, the Pool of London. It isn't a pool. It is a section of the Thames River that stretches from London Bridge to below Limehouse. Tall ships could navigate the pool up to London Bridge. The Pool of London is divided into two parts, the Upper Pool, and the Lower Pool. The Upper Pool consists of the section between London Bridge, which blocked tall masts from continuing west, and the Cherry Garden Pier in Bermondsey. The Lower Pool runs from the Cherry Garden Pier to Limekiln Creek. The pilot maneuvered the ship into a slip between two other ships remarkably similar to *Victory*. As we secured the lines and put out the gangplank, I noticed two men who seemed very eager to come aboard. I wondered who they were and why they were in such a hurry. Mr. Larsen told me they were tea buyers and they wanted to get our cargo of tea before anyone could get ahead of them. The captain knew them and invited them to his cabin.

The crew started offloading as soon as the dock lines were secured. Almost as soon as the gang plank went down, wagons were pulling up to receive the tea chests. The wagons would take them to one of many tea warehouses on the docks. Mr. Larsen said that sometimes the tea would go to an auction house. But he said the captain had already sold the tea to the two men who had come aboard when we docked.

It was not until the following afternoon that Sean and I got to go ashore. The place was teaming with wagons, horses, barrels, hogsheads, wood crates, sailors, and well-dressed folks. It was very noisy.

There were wagons of fruits, vegetables, sacks of grain, barrels of spices, bales of cotton, tobacco, and just about anything that could be imported. We even saw some exotic animals in cages, some cows, and sheep.

Mr. Larsen warned us to watch out for pickpockets who, he said, could steal your wallet without your ever knowing it. We had not had lunch before we left the ship, so Sean and I were hungry. We smelled it before we found it, a little shop with a big red sign that read "Fish and Chips." We ordered two portions that came wrapped in brown paper. Fish and Chips: deep-fried cod fish and fried potatoes. It was delicious.

We had enough time for some sightseeing. The first place we looked at was Smithfield. It struck me as being old. When I read the plaque, it confirmed my suspicion. A place of execution for over 400 years, Smithfield took its name from "smooth field," a grassy space just outside the city walls. A horse market in the Middle Ages, Smithfield was also a prime location for battles, tournaments, and merrymaking alike, hosting the debauched Bartholomew Fair for over 700 years. There, rebels, criminals, witches, and heretics were burned, roasted, or boiled alive.

The local shops sold porcelain, tea, lots and lots of silver, and furniture. We investigated the front window of a shop that had several men making cigars. Some of the boxes on display were marked "Ketcherell's, Virginia," and others "Havana." At one point Sean and I wandered into a great hall where *there* were lots of men and a great many skillfully placed piles of tobacco. I recognized the sweet-smelling aroma from my dad's pipe tobacco. Dad kept a small wooden cask on his desk that was marked "Orinoco." Sometimes he would let me fill his old wooden pipe. I remember my dad really enjoyed smoking his pipe after dinner.

Sean and I watched as the group moved slowly through the piles of tobacco and hogsheads. There was one man who was the auctioneer and the others were buyers. The auctioneer shouted a singsong of numbers, then suddenly stopped and shouted "Sold" when one of the men in the group put up his hand. It was fun to watch as we moved along with the group from pile to pile. Several of the piles were marked with names like Ford's Virginia and James River. That was tobacco from America. Mr. Larsen told me that England was a "free trade" country and that made it a good place to do business. Through Smithfield, he said, the British imported many of the raw materials they consumed before the gallows were moved to Tyburn in the 15th century. Yet even without the gallows, Smithfield was a magnet for violence, earning the moniker 'Ruffians Hall' in the 17th century. The area soon became a cattle market, and conditions only worsened, with cattle slaughtered in the market and animal entrails filling draining channels. The London Central Meat Market opened in 1868.

Next, we visited Westminster Abbey. My neck started to hurt from straining to see the ceiling and the stained glass. An old priest at the door greeted us. He asked where we were from and if we would like him to show us around the Abbey. I asked how much that would cost and he said with a hearty laugh, "If you say a little prayer for me one day, that will be sufficient." He told us Westminster Abbey had a prime role in London's history. Some say that the very first church on nearby Thorney Island existed in the 7th century. King Offa of Mercia granted land to 'St Peter and the needy people of God in Thorney in the terrible place which is called Westminster." So, when Edward the Confessor began building Westminster Abbey, there was already a church there. Over time, Westminster Abbey rose in grandeur and importance with William I crowned there in 1066. Our guide showed us where generations of British royalty had been buried. When the tour was over, as we thanked him, he asked if we went to church. I told him I had always gone to church before I went to sea. My mom had long ago told me the story of King Henry VIII, so I wasn't going to tell him I was Catholic, but he never asked. Then he gave us both a blessing and recommended we go see Trafalgar Square. We headed there next. It was a bit of a hike but worth it. The first thing visible was the column above the houses ahead long before we reached the square. The column is a monument to Horatio Nelson, said to be the greatest of English naval heroes. It was built to commemorate Britain's triumph over France. Lord Nelson was killed at the Battle of Trafalgar in 1805, in which the Royal Navy defeated a combined force of 33 French and Spanish ships, destroying about 20, without itself losing a single ship.

The monument, designed by William Railton, was built between 1840 and 1843. Lord Nelson's statue, 18 feet (5.5 m) high and sculpted of sandstone by Edward Hodges Baily, surveys Trafalgar Square from the top of a fluted granite column, and the entire monument measures 169 feet (51.59 m). The column is capped by bronze sculptural elements cast from melted cannon barrels from the wreckage of an 18th-century British warship. A few days before the statue was hoisted into place, a party of fourteen people ate a perilous steak dinner on top of the column. The base of the column features four bronze reliefs of Nelson's naval victories that were added between 1849 and 1854.

It was getting late, but Sean wanted to see the changing of the guard. He asked a policeman who told him he would have to come back in the morning to see it. We were pretty tired, so we headed back to the ship. The next morning, we asked the mate if we could spend another day sightseeing and he agreed. We arrived at Buckingham Palace in plenty of time to see the changing of the guard. While we waited, we bought a little pamphlet that explained what the changing of the guard was all about. It said the changing of the guard occurs across three locations: Buckingham Palace, St James's Palace, and Wellington Barracks, located only 275 meters from Buckingham Palace. It is a ceremony whereby the Old Guard leave St James's Palace, the most senior royal palace in the UK, to relieve the Guard at Buckingham Palace. When they appeared, Sean was delighted. He said he had never seen anything like the uniforms of the guardsmen, especially their hats, described as bearskins. The pamphlet informed us "Britain adopted the bearskin in 1768 to distinguish their grenadiers on the battlefield and in military parades. British grenadiers, an elite group of soldiers known for their strength and named for throwing grenades, limited their use of the bearskin to ceremonies at home because its fur deteriorated during overseas travel. The Queen's Guard is responsible for guarding St. James' Palace as well as Buckingham Palace in London."

Lots of steamboats sailed the Thames River. Mr. Larsen talked about steamboats and Mr. Fulton's steamboat that was running on the Hudson River in New York. He said he had seen steam fueled farm tractors on some farms in England. And he predicted that one day they could be made to power big ships.

13

WITH OUR HOLD jam packed with all sorts of cargo for New York and provisions for a long journey, we sailed out of the Thames and began the long journey home. Going from London to New York could take a month if the weather was good and a lot more than that if we ran into bad weather. Fortunately, the weather was very good, and we had only two or three days of calm and about the same number of storms. I got to steer the ship a lot and learned more and more about the names of the sails and how they were used. I learned the names of most of the lines they used to raise and lower the sails. And I was learning why changes in the sails were ordered as the weather changed. Why some sails were lowered in heavy weather and why more sails were added in calm weather. I found it fascinating. While we were in London I bought a notebook and pencil and started making notes about what I learned every day about sailing. Every time the captain or Mr. Larsen gave a command, I memorized it and wrote it in my notebook that night.

It was great to see that the land we knew was America. Then before long we sailed into the Narrow in New York and took on a pilot. He guided our ship to a slip on South Street in New York City. Once again, our ship was docked along with dozens of other sailing ships from ports around the world. When you looked along South Street there were rows and rows of ship masts as far as you could see. Almost as soon as we docked, the crew started unloading our cargo. It was a wonderful feeling to be home again and to have learned so much about the sea in the year and a half we were gone. I had already seen a lot of the world and I wasn't yet sixteen years old. Imagine, I had been to China, Hawaii, England, and Valparaiso, places my sister had probably never even heard of. I wondered what my old school friend Thomas would say if I could tell him about my adventures. I bet he would have loved to hear about the little steamboat I saw in London.

Mr. Larsen said we would probably be in New York for about a month and that we would be getting our pay in a day or two just as soon as the cargo was offloaded, and the buyers paid for their cargo. The captain left the ship after a few days. Mr. Larsen was in charge, and Sean and I were eager to explore the seaport, especially now that we would have some money to spend. Once the cargo was unloaded most of the crew left the ship. I wondered how many of them would return. Mr. Larsen said we could stay aboard and if we wanted to go on the next voyage, he would be happy to sign us up for it. We were both good cabin boys, he said. He did not know where our next trip would be; that would depend on what our cargo was and where it had to go.

The first place we headed for was just a few blocks along South Street, the Fulton Fish Market. Mr. Larsen said that all kinds of fish from far and near come to be sold at the Fulton Fish Market. There were a great many restaurants and fish stores in New York City, and they all got their fish from the Fulton Fish Market. We arrived fairly late, and it was just beginning to get busy. The fish markets are in full swing just about the time everyone else is getting up. Men were hauling ice to put on the tables. Fish of every description were out there, many still squirming. There was a big fish with a kind of long pointy spout, a swordfish. Lots of big turtles, big chunks of tuna and cod fish, shrimp, oysters, clams, mussels, scallops, eels, crabs, and sardines covered the tables. I did not know the names, but they had little signs stuck in the chopped ice. I saw so many fish I had never heard of that I vowed I would try one day to find a book that described them.

At the rear of the market, there was a booth where a man was selling New England clam chowder. Sean and I both ordered a bowl and sat down by the bulkhead to eat our soup. It was piping hot and delicious, with chopped pieces of clams. The man gave us both some little crackers to eat with our chowder. In the following days, we tried all kinds of foods we had never had before. We did a lot of walking in New York. One day we walked along Broadway and visited a very old Trinity Church. The dark red sandstone building dated back to the 1680s. It had been destroyed by fire and rebuilt three or four times. Buried in its cemetery were those I had read about in school: Robert Fulton, Alexander Hamilton, Captain James Lawrence, and Hercules Mulligan. My dad told me about Mr. Mulligan, one of those cold winter evenings in Ohio when we all sat around the fire listening to Dad tell stories.

We walked up Broadway past some beautiful mansions as far as it went until it became farmland. One place I especially enjoyed was P.T. Barnum's American Museum right there on Broadway at Park Row and Anne Streets. It was a five-story building that the guide told me was once a natural history museum called the Scudders American Museum. A placard in the lobby told the story. In 1841 Mr. Barnum acquired the building and changed it into a combination zoo, museum, lecture hall, wax museum, theater, and freak show. Barnum filled the American Museum with diorama, panoramas, "cosmoramas", scientific instruments, modern appliances, a Flea circus, a loom powered by a dog, the trunk of a tree under which Jesus' disciples sat, an oyster bar, a rifle range, waxworks, glass blowers, taxidermists, a phrenologist, a pretty baby contests, Ned the learned seal, the Fiji Merman (a mummified monkey's torso with a fish's tail), midgets, Chang and Eng a pair of Siamese twins, a menagerie of exotic animals that included beluga whales in an aquarium, giants, Native Americans who performed traditional songs and dances, Grizzly Adams's trained bears, and performances ranging from magicians, ventriloquists, and blackface minstrels to adaptations of biblical tales and Uncle Tom's Cabin. I was not sure what a ventriloquist was, and I was happy to find out that they were talented and a lot of fun. Sean got a big kick out of what was billed as a mermaid. To me, it looked like a shriveled-up old fish with a doll's head on it. The ship stayed at the slip on South Street for a few weeks for repairs and some new sails. I wanted to get the present I had bought for my mom mailed to them. I bought a Meerschaum pipe for my dad. For my brother, I bought a sperm whale tooth with scrimshawed images of whales and a whale ship from a whaleman. I asked where I could find a post office and was told there was a post office nearby. I wrapped the gifts in some old sail canvas and mailed them to my family. Then a day later Mr. Larsen told us we were going to be loading cargo for Havana, Cuba.

He said he had been to Cuba several times and thought we would probably careen the ship while we were there. He explained that from time to time a ship had to have its bottom scraped and tarred. Often, he said, some of the wood that was under water most of the time needed to be repaired. To protect the hull from rot and woodworms. To do that they had to get the ship to gently settle on the sand and roll over to one side on its keel. Mr. Larsen called the process careening. This is done at a port called *de Cardenas*. The bay is particularly good and can host many ships. They have a setup where once the ship is in place and the tide starts to go out, lines are attached to the masts and the ship is pulled over so that when it settles to the sand one whole half of the hull is out of the water and can be repaired. It seemed to me to be an exciting thing to see, and I was eager to set sail for Havana.

14

WHILE THERE IN New York in 1861 we heard about how the Confederates had fired on Fort Sumpter and how Mr. Lincoln had declared that the Union was at war. Sean and I wondered if we should join the Union Army. Mr. Larsen said that it was more important for us to learn the ways of the sea and perhaps one day when we were experienced seamen, join the Union Navy. He thought the war would go on for a long time.

Mail took a long time to catch up with ships. It was not until a year after I heard about the Civil War that I got a letter from my mom. My younger brother John had joined the 17th Ohio Volunteer Infantry Regiment. Somehow, I knew he would. Mom wrote that he had been assigned to guard railroad trains. She was relieved that he was not in the actual battles that had taken the lives of neighbors. Sometime after Mom's letter, I received a letter from John in a sack of mail we exchanged with a passing ship. By then John was in the thick of it and was already fighting. John wrote,

Dear Patrick,

By now I guess mom has told you that I joined 17th Ohio. I lied about my age, but they did not seem too worried about it. Mom and Bertha were in tears and begged me not to go but Dad said he understood why I wanted to go. He said he wished he could go too. The army sent a wagon to pick me up, and some other boys up then took us all to Camp Dennison in Cincinnati. They gave me a uniform and taught us how to drill and use a bayonet. They gave me an Enfield musket and warned me that if I lost it, I would have to pay for it. We did some shooting at the firing range, but they said I was dam good shot and I did not really ready much training. They gave me a little badge that said I was a sharpshooter, and they gave me a different rifle called a Sharps. It was a sweet little rife. The sergeant told me it was going to be my best friend. I thank you and dad for teaching me how to shoot. I was not sure how I would be when I would have to shoot another person. Deer and squirrels are one thing but shooting another human being is something I dreaded. The sergeant told us not to worry. He said that "When the Johnny Rebs start shooting at you and you hear them bullets whistling over your head, you won't have no problem shootin' back." In about a month we got shipped to Camp Dick Robinson in Kentucky. I sure had done a lot of walking by then, but it wasn't so bad. The army gave me the best boots I ever had. My first taste of battle happened at a place called Wild Cat, Kentucky.

We ran smack into a bunch of Johhny Rebs hiding in a field. All hell broke loose, and bullets were screaming over our heads, smoke filled the air, and the place stunk of blood, guts, and exploded gunpowder. Seven of our boys were killed and a bunch were wounded. But we beat the Rebs back until they were running into the woods like scared rabbits. I couldn't blame the poor bastards. I was scared as hell too. Then the next thing you know we were part of the 31st Regiment Ohio Volunteer Infantry and the 38th Regiment Ohio Volunteer Infantry. It's funny how when you are in the middle of a fight you don't much think about dying because you're too busy staying alive. But then when there is some quiet and after you have some chow, you get to thinking about what happens if you catch one of those Reb bullets. It is not so much fear, it is more trying to figure out how you would accept what could very possibly happen at any moment. How would Mom take it? Would they get my body back home or would they just bury me there like I helped them do when my buddies got it? Then the next morning it starts all over again and you're back to surviving. Then we fought in Kentucky at Louisville and then Lebanon. Then I got my first ride on a riverboat. It was the Magnolia headed from Nashville, Tennessee traveling on the Ohio and Cumberland Rivers. We fought so many battles in so many places I can't remember them all. One I will never forget, is Chickamauga, Tennessee. The Rebs got the best of us, and I was shot a bullet in the leg. It hurt like nothing I have ever felt before. They took me to a place where the wounded were screaming. I was damn sure they were going to saw off my leg but somehow, maybe it was the prayers I was repeating over and over in my head. I guess it wasn't as bad as I thought because they did not take my leg. They said the war was over for me and sent me home. I sure wish they had let me keep the Sharps rifle, but I had to turn it in. They did let me keep my Kapi hat and my uniform boots and all. I guess the bullet hole in my pants leg made them unfit for further use. So, brother, I am writing this from a military hospital back where I started from at Camp Denison. The food is great, the beds are comfortable and most of the nurses are beautiful young women who could not be nicer. My leg is feeling much better, but they tell me it will be a long while before it is healed. They keep worrying about something they call gangrene. Keep coming in and putting on what a nurse told me is pure bromine. All I know is that it hurts like hell. They say it is going to cure me if it doesn't kill me.

Your loving brother
John"

I joined the 13th Regiment NY Cavalry on June 11th, 1862 in New York City. I mustered in as a private in Company A on June 19th, 1862. I signed up for three years. On August 17th, 1865, I was transferred to Company G of the Third New York Provisional Cavalry.

15

WE SET SAIL for Havana with a cargo hold that was filled with a large variety of goods. Some of the same things we brought from China were loaded destined for Havana. Mr. Larsen said that Cuba had to import many things because their main industry was sugar. We were going to load mainly sugar and Havana cigars to bring to England. Mr. Larsen said that Havana was a center of the slave trade. He told us the captain would never consider transporting slaves. And Mr. Larsen agreed that it just was not right what they were doing to those people. He said what made him angry was that a lot of the slave trade ship captains were Africans who were selling their own people into the misery of slavery. We did see a slave market there in Havana and a slave ship. The passage to Cuba was uneventful, but our trip to London was very rough. In fact, in one of the several storms we encountered, one of the crewmen fell from the yards while trying to reel a sail in through while he battles to stay aloft during high waves and strong winds. He died when his body hit the deck. It was a bloody mess. Sean and I helped to scrub the deck clean of his blood. We buried him at sea. They wrapped his body in burlap and put some stones from the bilge blast into the sack. The captain said some words as crewmen dumped his body into the water. Everyone was sad about it for the next week. Once again, we sailed into the Thames River and tied up.

I made several voyages on the *Victory*. By the time I was 21 years old, I was an able-bodied seaman and by 24, I was third mate. Mr. Abraham Lincoln was president of the United States. I knew dad had voted for him, so I figured he must be a good man. All my studies of how to use the sextant, plot a chart and control of the sails had paid off. I had read every one of the books the captain had lent me about seamanship.

In 1865, I heard from a cabin boy on an American ship we were berthed with that the Confederate General Robert E. Lee had surrendered at Appomattox courthouse in Virginia. The war that had pitted brother against brother was over. I found it hard to understand what this civil war was all about. I had seen African slaves on some of the slave ships we encountered. My captain and first mate both hated the idea and would never be involved in the slave trade. Yet it was my understanding that George Washington, Thomas Jefferson and many other American patriots who signed the Declaration of Independence had owned slaves. Mr. Larsen said there was a lot more to it than just the issue of slavery. He explained that a friend of his from Alabama said it all started with the cotton gin. He said that farmers in the South were not doing so well with their cotton. It was hard, hot work picking cotton. And it tore your fingers apart picking the cotton out of thorny pods. Many plantation owners were reducing the number of slaves that were needed to pick cotton. Then along came Mr. Eli Whitney with his invention of a cotton gin. It was a device that separated the seeds from raw cotton. Suddenly, a process that was extraordinarily labor-intensive could be completed quickly and easily. By the early 1800s, cotton emerged as the South's major cash crop. Tobacco, rice, and sugar declined in popularity. Cotton became king and the need for slaves grew rapidly. Those states that depended on slave labor were not about to give it up because some Yankees suddenly wanted to free the slaves. After all, they reasoned, slavery had been around since 3500 BC, so why, suddenly, did it need to be abolished. Didn't George Washington have slaves? The Southern states were not going to stand for anyone taking away their slaves and their wealth just to make colored people equal.

I had not known much about slavery other than seeing slaves on ships and in slave markets. My revulsion against slavery drove me to the point where I did not want to even think about it. That changed when I came across a used book at a stall in London. *Uncle Toms Cabin* by Harriet Beecher Stowe was a fascinating and shocking account of the life of a slave in America. Uncle Tom is a dignified, good and noble man, steadfast his beliefs. He is being taken to a slave market by boat to New Orleans. An accident occurs and Tom manages to save the life of a girl named Eva who is the daughter of the man who bought Tom at the auction. Eva is grateful for her rescue and befriends Tom. She is very sickly, and, on her deathbed, she pleads with her father to free Tom and all the slaves he owns. Her father agrees, but is killed before he can do so, possibly because neighbors heard of his intention. Enter Simon Legree, the man that bought Tom from Eva's dad when he bought the farm. Legree is a cruel, sadistic man and a ruthless slave owner. He whips Tom to death because he refuses to tell Legree where a group of escaped slaves are hiding.

Like people around the world, I was enlightened, sickened and engaged by an accurate portrayal of atrocities many slaves suffered. The book, I am told, played an important part in persuading people that slavery had to be abolished.

16

THE FOLLOWING YEAR Captain Livingstone retired, and I found a berth as third mate on another ship. The ship was very similar to the *Victory*. She was named *American Pride*. Her captain was John Foresight from Maine; the first mate was Seamus from Ireland. Like me, he had red hair and a red beard. He hated the nickname "Red" and let me know it. I told Seamus I felt the same way and we hit off very well right from the start. Seamus assumed I was born in Ireland and was quite surprised when I told him that I was born on a farm in Milan, a small town near Celina, Ohio, as was my dad. I learned a great deal from Seamus. In fact, he saved my life. We were heading to Havana when we got into a bad storm. The wind was so strong it snapped off our main mast and it, along with the yards and the sails, crashed onto the deck. Seamus heard the mast crack and pulled me out of the way just in time, for surely it would have crushed me to death right there near the binnacle. As it was, the mast killed two crewmen and smashed the helm and compass. On another voyage I made with Seamus, I returned the favor when he got into an argument with a nasty fellow who was threatening to kill him over his portion of rum. The sailor had somehow gotten into the barrel of rum that was kept on deck and was obviously very drunk. When I spotted them, the crewman was swinging a large knife at Seamus who was armed with nothing more than a belaying pin. I picked up a coil of rope and threw it at the crew member. It hit him in the face, which gave Seamus time to move in and hit him with the belaying pin and knock him unconscious.

Word of the battle of Bull Run reached us before we left Liverpool."

Seamus and I sailed together on a dozen voyages to places like Cuba, Valparaiso, France, Holland, and Venice. When Seamus was promoted to captain after our captain died of a heart attack, he made me his first mate. I remember fondly our voyage to Venice, Italy. It was an enchanting place; the main streets were canals. People got around in boats they called "gondolas," rowed usually by one man standing in the back of the boat. Some of the gondolas had one man in the front and one in the rear. The gondoliers wore straw hats and striped knitted shirts. Some of the gondolas were covered and privately owned by some of the very rich residents of Venice. We strolled up one canal then over a small foot bridge then down another canal and quite by accident looked across the canal and saw a boat yard for gondolas. The *squero* is next to the Campo San Treviso and the San Treviso Church in the Dorsoduro section of Venice. It is a traditional boatyard, one of the oldest in the city. One of the shipwrights we talked to told us that at one time there were more than 10,000 Venetian vessels plying the city's waters and were the primary mode of transport. Around 60 boat builders were employed by the *squero* during this prosperous period. We watched as the skilled craftsmen cut ribs and planks and placed them in a jig the shipwright told us had been in the shop for at least a hundred years. In another area a man was fitting leather to the deck of a gondola. He explained that gondolas are built in the shape of a banana, not with a straight keel like on any other boat. It made sense when he described how rowing on one side of boat would make it steer to the side. By making the boat curved, the rower need only row on the one side to have the boat go straight.

In yet another part of the yard, the gondolas were being lacquered a shiny black. We learned that the decoration of the gondolas was made by different guilds. The *furcula*, which is actually the oarlock that has to be designed for each individual gondolier, and oars were made by skilled wood carvers. The metal decorations were made by another. And the traditional striped shirts, straw hats and other clothing were the province of yet another guild.

Seamus told me that every one of the many beautiful buildings and churches in Venice was built on wooden pilings driven into the ground. While we were docked in Venice one time, a friend of Seamus who was in the ship building business took us on a tour of a place called the *Arsenale*. It was a massive ship building factory where at one time a 300-foot merchant ship was built in one day. Venice was for a time the trading center of Europe. Riches from around the world flowed through Venice. However, Napoleon Bonaparte invaded Venice and destroyed the place and the ship under construction fearing that it could build ships to fight against his navy.

I had a ride in a gondola and I fell in love with Venice. The restaurants along the Grand Canal were wonderful, as were the shops. On one of our voyages to Venice, Seamus and I found ourselves right in the middle of what the Venetians called *Carnevale*. It is a party that goes on for weeks and fills the square with people dressed in costumes and masks. There is a lot of drinking, dancing, music, and wild behavior. It was delightful. I think I was kissed by at least a dozen masked women I had never met.

There were some wonderful leather shops along the canals. There were shops that sold some of the finest linen I had seen anywhere in the world. In one of the islands in the lagoon called Murano there are dozens of glass blowers. I was amazed to see how skilled artisans heated glass tubes and blew into to them to form bowls, vases and just about anything shape they could imagine. There were also lots and lots of glass beaded jewelry on sale in Murano.

St Mark's Cathedral, the grand religious and architectural center of Venice was awesome. High above its main entrance, were four bronze statues of horses, so realistic that you might assume they were real, except they stood perfectly still. St Mark's was beautiful and filled with art works. I was amazed too when the guide pointed out to us water marks on the wall of the cathedral that he explained were left by the seawater. He said that sometimes the sea invades Venice during what he called *Aqua Alta* to the point where at times there was six feet of water in the cathedral. The square out front was totally flooded and people had to move their furniture to the second floor of their homes along the canals and inland. I returned to Venice as often as I could. I loved visiting the many churches and seeing the incredibly beautiful works of art that seemed to be in just about every church and cathedral I visited. I saw my first opera in the beautifully decorated *Teatro La Fenice* theater in Venice.

On a voyage to Genoa, Italy, we had a longer than normal layover, while waiting to get enough cargo to make our next trip worthwhile. The shipping agents dealt with that while I took myself a little time for touring the beautiful and historical country that is Italy. It probably sounds somewhat macabre, but I do enjoy visiting cemeteries. My first stop in Genoa was a cemetery, *Cimiterio Monumentale di Staglieno* The Staglieno Cemetery as it is called in English, is overflowing with beautiful lifelike sculptures.

The cemetery so impressed Mark Twain when he visited there, he wrote,

> "We shall continue to remember it after we shall have forgotten the palaces. It is a vast marble colonnaded corridor extending around a great unoccupied square of ground: its broad floor is marble, and on every slab is an inscription--for every slab covers a corpse. On either side, as one walks down the middle of the passage, are monuments, tombs, and sculptured figures that are exquisitely wrought and are full of grace and beauty. They are new and snowy: every outline is perfect, every feature guiltless of mutilation, flaw, or blemish; forms; and therefore, to use these far-reaching ranks of bewitching forms are a hundred-fold more lovely than the damaged and dingy statuary they saved from the wreck of ancient art set up in the galleries of Paris for the worship of the world."

I think of the many impressive sculptures I viewed, the tomb of Caterina Campodonico was the most impressive. It features a lifelike statue of Caterina Campodonico, a peasant nut-seller who saved all of her money to build a lavish tomb. The statue depicts her holding a string of walnuts as she did in life.

I took a train from Genoa to Rome. My goal was to see Rome and the Vatican. A man I chatted with on the train warned me to be aware of pickpockets. Sure, enough I encountered a few as I was leaving the station in Rome. They are very quick and very tricky. One I encountered was a young boy who held a carboard sign over his other hand, I am not sure what the sign read, because the writing was not English. I watched one of the pickpockets grab a gentlemen's pocket watch so quickly the man never realized what was happening. The thief was gone in an instant. The following day I observed a team of thieves. A woman bumped into a gentleman and while he was apologizing the other thief reached into the man's pocket and stole his wallet. Fortunately, I was never robbed.

I visited most of the major sights like the Coliseum and the Trevi fountain. The Vatican was my favorite. From the Sistine chapel to the majesty of the St. Peters Cathedral, it was breathtaking. I had a good laugh at a little nun whose job it was to make sure no one entered St Peter's unless they were appropriately dressed. The little nun was trying to explain to a very large Russian woman, who was broad in the beam and wearing a very revealing shirt, that she was not permitted to enter without the proper clothing. The little nun blocked the Russian woman from entering, and an argument ensued with lots of shouting on the part of the Russian woman. In no time two very tall Carabinieri arrived and ended the argument. The Russian woman ambled away from the entrance muttering what I perceived to be some serious Russian profanity.

Even the bridge leading to the Vatican was built by the Romans thousands of years ago. The beauty of Michelangelo's ceiling in the Sistine Chapel is beyond my ability to describe it. The columns around the altar were sheer beauty as were the many side altars. My absolute favorite was *The Pièta*, Michelangelo's beautiful statue of the Blessed Mother Mary cradling a dying Christ in her arms. The detail and almost human features of the statue are magnificent.

From Rome I traveled to Florence which I had heard was a wonderful city. Of all the wonders of Florence I think the Cathedral of Santa Maria del Fiore was the most impressive. The guide explained that construction of the cathedral was begun in 1296, but the dome was not completed until 1436. It took one hundred and forty years to find the right man, a goldsmith turned architectural genius, Filippo Brunelleschi, who was able to construct a dome 100 feet in diameter without the use of wooden scaffolding. I got to actually climb up into the space between the inner and outer walls of the dome. Getting the lantern built on top of the dome and getting the dome to stay up was truly astounding. Santa

Maria del Fiore is one of the largest churches in the world. Its history is fascinating. The plan consists of a triple-nave with the presbytery area nested within and dominated by the large octagon of the immense dome. Surrounding the dome are five chapels. The building is five hundred and two feet in length, two hundred ninety feet wide at the transept and three hundred seventy-five feet high from the floor to the base of the dome lantern. The name Santa Maria del Fiore refers to the name of the city, the city of flowers.

From an American tourist, we heard that President Lincoln had signed the Emancipation Proclamation, something I thought was long overdue. I had seen many slaves and encountered several slave ships. I was horrified at the slave markets I had seen in Haiti and elsewhere. I remember reading Lincoln's Gettysburg address and thought how awful it must have been. Brother against brother, most of whom really did not know what caused the war. All they knew was they loved their country and paid the ultimate price for their patriotism. I was struck by a speech he gave in which he said, "Freedom has given us the control of 200,000 able bodied men, born and raised on southern soil. It will give us more yet. Just so much it has subtracted from the strength of our enemies, and instead of alienating the South from us there are evidences of a fraternal feeling growing between our own and rebel soldiers. My enemies condemn my emancipation policy. Let them prove by the history of this war, that we can restore the Union without it."

A T ONE POINT I had a layover in New York while the agents were gathering cargo. I was never one to waste time when a ship was idle. I took advantage of learning about whatever country I was in. I visited shops, especially bookshops, and did a lot of sightseeing. One afternoon I read in the paper that the public was invited to see a demonstration of the new telegraph. It sounded interesting so I arranged to attend. It was held in a small theater in the financial district. I found myself a seat up front. A man introduced himself as Samuel Laws, President of the Gold Indicator Company. He made a few remarks, then introduced a man who was sitting on stage. At first the man, who was about my age, seemed as if he was ignoring the introduction, then as the speaker tapped on his shoulder the man stood up. The host said, "I give you Mr. Thomas Edison." Recognizing the name of my boyhood friend, I wondered could this man possibly be the same Tom I spent so much time with as a boy growing up back in Michigan. Tom talked about modern telegraphy and how it enabled instant communication between widely separated offices, cities and even countries. He explained that his first patent was for the electric vote recorder, He said it worked very well, but no one was interested, "So I moved to New York to find someone who might be interested." He said one of the people I learned from was a fellow telegrapher and inventor named Franklin Leonard Pope. He said Mr. Pope was a good friend and one of his mentors during those early years, Tom said that when times were tough, Pope allowed him to live and work in the basement of his Elizabeth, New Jersey home. Then Tom said he joined up with a man name Samuel Laws at the Gold Indicator Company. Tom went on to demonstrate his improved telegraph device. After the presentation was over, I went up to talk to Tom. At first, he did not seem to remember me. I soon realized that Tom was hard of hearing. He encouraged me to speak up. Then it dawned on him. His eyes lit up and he broke into a big smile. He gave me a big hug and insisted that we have lunch together. He invited Mr. Laws to join us, and we took a carriage to Delmonico's restaurant. I had never heard of it, but I soon discovered it was quite an incredible place. Delmonico's ` consisted of three floors and private dining rooms. Mr. Laws said that he was told the pillars had been imported from Pompeii in 1837. He said that it was the watering hole for wealthy people and well-off foreigners and many of the Americans amassing fortunes. It had the reputation as being one of the finest restaurants in New York. It was obvious that Mr. Laws was a regular diner at Delmonico's. He explained that he often hosted meetings at the restaurant for the annual gathering of the New England Society of New York, which featured many important speakers of the day. Laws said he had attended an event at the Academy of Music on east 14ᵗʰ street that was catered by Delmonico's. It was to welcome Queen Victoria and the Prince of Wales. Supper was set out in a specially constructed room; the menu was French, and it included my favorite Mousse au chocolate, fashioned in the likeness of Queen Vitoria and Prince Albert. I had no idea what pièces montées were, so I asked Mr. Laws to explain. He said he didn't know at the time either when he saw it on the menu. He said that when it was served, he discovered it was an elaborate hand constructed dessert in the image of the royals. We stayed quite a while after Mr. Laws left. Fortunately, he told the waiter to put the tab on his bill including "anything my guests desire after I leave." I was relieved to hear that because I wasn't sure if Tom could afford it and I was damn well sure it was way over my head. Tom and I reminisced about our childhood. He told me he now lived in Gramercy Park in New York city. We laughed about some of his chemistry experiments that ended up with a bang and very often a scolding for us both from his mom. He recalled missing school a lot, which I remembered, when as a young boy when he developed scarlet fever. I asked him where he moved to after he left Ohio, Tom said that in 1854 his family moved to Port Huron, Michigan. Then in 1874 he developed a telegraph machine that could send two messages simultaneously. Tom and I agreed to meet again after my next voyage.

18

MY NEXT VOYAGE was fairly routine, New York to Limerick. The weather was good, and the seas were calm. A few months later I was back in New York. Thomas invited me to come out to Menlo Park in Middlesex County, New Jersey. He was eager to show me his new laboratory. Tom was truly in his element. He and his staff were working on a variety of inventions including the telephone, phonograph, electric railway, iron ore separation, electric lighting, and voice recording. After the tour, Tom escorted me to his office. He sat at his very cluttered desk and sat back in his big oak desk chair while I sat opposite. There was a plaque on his desk with a quotation which read "There is no expedient to which man will not resort to avoid the real labor of thinking." Tom inquired about my latest voyage, then asked if I had one of the John Harrison Longitude clocks. I was a little surprised that he knew about a device that was probably as important to navigation as the compass. I explained that I did indeed have one. He asked why it was important. I told Tom that before John Harrison's longitude clock, mariners had a great deal of trouble trying to keep accurate time, and therefore had difficulty finding what longitude they were in. I was very familiar with the work of John Harrison, and I described to Tom why it was so important. Before the 18th century, ocean navigators could not find an accurate way of determining longitude. There were some enormous clocks the size of a casket. They were expensive, troublesome, and difficult to use. Then along came a man who had trained as a carpenter but had a passion for clocks. John Harrison solved one of the most difficult problems of his time by creating an accurate and practical chronometer. The best scientists of the time, including Sir Isaac Newton, thought it impossible. Harrison spent four decades perfecting a clock that would earn him compensation from Parliament. His accomplishment was unfairly blocked by some jealous scientists of the time, until he was finally recognized by the intervention of King George III of Great Britain who was himself an inventor. I promised that the next time we met I would bring along my longitude chronometer. Tom and I remained friends and exchanged Christmas cards. From time to time when he had an event in New York City we would meet for lunch or dinner.

19

ON ONE VOYAGE from New York to Liverpool the North Atlantic was particularly nasty. We were driven north more than a hundred miles by fierce storms. About two weeks out it finally calmed, and we were making good speed. The lookout high up in crow's nest shouted out "small boat ho. " I looked where he was pointing and saw nothing. We reefed sail and in a brief time came upon two dories like the one I had seen on whale ships. The mate and his crew lowered the longboat, and I sent a crew out to rescue the poor souls that looked like they were almost dead. Once the men were safely onboard, we retrieved the longboat and hoisted sail again. Cookie brewed them up some hot broth which they sipped quietly and rested for a few hours.

The men were badly sun burned, their lips were swollen and their hair was matted and salty as were their beards. In a day or two they had recovered well enough to start eating real food, which they relished. One of the men identified himself as Christopher Foxworthy, the Captain . I invited Foxworthy to my cabin as soon as he was well enough, and we talked for several hours.

He told his story. They were whalers out of Nantucket. Hunting had been particularly good and their hold was nearly filled with whale oil. Then late one night they heard a thud that seemed to be right under his cabin. A few moments later there was another thud. Then it stopped. The following day they caught their last whale and drew it alongside for processing. The crew was at the kettles boiling down the blubber when suddenly a giant sperm whale shot almost straight up and put of the water about fifty feet of the starboard bow. He was close enough, the captain said, that I could see his eye looking at us. Foxworthy told me they were nearly finished cutting out when he heard a thud that seemed to be on the portside. A second thud lifted the ship out of the water. By then he knew a whale was attacking the ship. Again, and again the whale slammed into the hull. One of the harpooners managed to plant his harpoon into the beast's head as it once again smashed into midships. The captain was weeping as he talked about his young son who was on his first voyage.

> When the whale attacked, he said, "My son was at my side. I managed to get him into one of the dories and we watched as the ship broached then quickly sank into the sea. It seemed as if the worst was over."

He described how suddenly the whale surfaced once again with two harpoons dangling from his head with blood gushing out of the wounds. The whale headed straight for the dories and smashed into one, sending its crew flying high in the air in a shower of splinting wood. Then all was calm for a few days as they floated on the open eerily quiet sea.

The captain said he was optimistic that they would soon see another whale ship or a ship like ours because they were in fairly well traveled waters. After a week they were beginning to feel the suffering. Water was running low and the provisions they managed to save were gone. They were becoming dehydrated and desperate. There were two dories separated by about fifty feet. When suddenly the whale surfaced again with harpoons dangling from his head. Pushing a bow wave ahead, the whale smashed into the captain's dory. They were thrown high in the air in a hail of wood and gear. The captain and his son managed to swim to the other dory as the whale disappeared. The boy had been badly injured in the attack. A few days later he died in his fathers' arms. Then for several days they drifted aimlessly on what were mercifully calm seas. Late one afternoon a shock of fear went through the survivors as they spotted the whale bob up to the surface. They soon realized the whale was not attacking. In fact, he just floated there apparently injured and dying. Sharks were swarming around the whale and taking bites out of his flesh. The captain reasoned that the loss of blood had finally killed the great whale. The water around the whale was red with blood which, the captain reasoned, had alerted the sharks to a free meal. In all there were five survivors and they all recovered quite well. In a few days they were eagerly helping the crew man the ship.

One of the survivors, a grey-haired old whaler asked to borrow a pocketknife, then proceeded to carve a whaling scene into one of the barrel covers he found in the hold. He was a very good wood carver and, in a few days, presented me with a carving depicting a whale leading in what was called a Nantucket Sleigh Ride after being harpooned. Along the bottom he carved the words, "A dead whale or a stove boat."

The whale ship captain explained that there were numerous stories in the folklore of Nantucket that told of whales attacking a ship. The word stove means to break in the side of a ship. He said he thought perhaps the most famous was the story of the whaleship *Essex*. *Essex*, was a whaler out of Nantucket that was rammed by a sperm whale on November 20, 1820, and later sank. Although all 20 crewmen initially survived, only eight were rescued following months adrift in the open sea. Their arduous journey drove them to the unthinkable last resort of cannibalism. The story was whispered about in Nantucket at a time of nostalgia when whalers gathered for a few pints. If a stranger asked about *Essex*, natives pleaded ignorance of the story. I learned another interesting thing from the whaler. He said they were always looking for ambergris. He explained that it is whale vomit that floats on the sea when the whale spits it out. He said it is like liquid gold because it is the basic ingredient in all the most expensive ladies' perfumes.

Once again we were back in Liverpool. I heard the great news that in April, 1865, General Lee surrendered at the Appomattox Court house in Virginia. At the same time we learned of the assassination of President Lincoln. I felt terrible and that got on my knees and prayed for the man I believed was the greatest president America ever had, just one notch above George Washington.

I had by then sailed with Seamus for a few years, then wound up as captain of a ship based in Limerick, Ireland, the *Ireland's Pride,* owned by one Liam Shanahan. Owner of three ships, Shanahan lived in Limerick. His ships carried everything from spices to tea to Limerick and brought a variety of goods including woolen clothing, Irish whiskey, and cheeses to all of Europe and America.

It was there in Limerick that I met the daughter of one of Mr. . Shanahan's friends. Nora Mary Adamson was a beautiful girl of seventeen. She captured my heart the moment I saw her. She had long auburn hair and features like a fine China doll. Her skin was smooth, clear, and beautiful. She could dance like no one I had ever known . I was a fair dancer but not as good as Nora. She could do all the latest dances. At parties she often wore tap shoes that clicked the rhythm of her Irish step dancing.. People cheered and clapped for her. She never tired.

20

ONE TIME WE were sailing to Spain when the lookout spotted a sailing vessel bearing down on us. I used my spyglass but could not quite recognize the ship. I was concerned about how she was heading. Generally, when you encounter a vessel at sea they remain on course as you do, unless you have reason to do otherwise. Always, a captain sailing those waters has to be aware of the possibility of being attacked by pirates. I had never been attacked by pirates, but had heard tales of those who had. The unknown ship kept gaining on us and got close enough to where we recognized her British flag. However, my mate pointed out that she was like no other British sailing vessel he had ever seen. I agreed and we immediately brought the arms on deck and distributed them to crew members. The officers, including myself, wore our side arms. We had a small cannon we used mainly for firing a line to another ship, but could also be loaded with scatter shot. We kept it hidden as the ship approached. When she got alarmingly close without identifying herself, we felt sure she was a privateer. A shot rang out from the ship. I had out some former military rifle men, one from Tennessee who was crack shot up in the rigging. The moment he heard the shot, he fired and incredibly hit the pirate captain in the forehead. I saw him fall as more shots rang out from my crew and from the pirates. I fired my pistol and watched a pirate fall. It looked like we were in for a battle and even boarding, until my first mate fired our little cannon. He managed to hit the main mast and we watched as the mast and sails hit the deck with a thunderous crash. There was screaming and lots of smoke. An incredible shot for even a large cannon. Then as if by magic, the pirate ship veered off to starboard. A cheer went up from our deck. I had heard that most of the pirates had been chased from that area, but obviously there were some still around. I ordered a few extra rations of rum for my crew and asked the cook to give them a special treat. He had been keeping a barrel of beef for a special occasion. We all feasted on an unusually tasty roast, potatoes, and gravy then we washed it down with plenty of rum.

I recall that after dinner we were all feeling fortunate and happy and perhaps well lubricated by the extra measures of rum. The crew got to telling stories. One of the old timers, a carpenter, entertained us with tales of his time in the Royal Navy. Henry told us about a time he was in a pub in Portsmouth having a grand old time with his mates. He said the rum was flowing freely and this kind gentleman was paying for the drinks. It seems the gentleman was celebrating his good fortune at the races, and wanted to share his joy with everyone. Henry said that he was having a gay old time of it when he noticed the gentleman drop a shilling coin into his tankard of rum.

At the time he said, "I thought that was right nice of him to make me a present of a shilling. As the evening went on I got myself very drunk and the gentleman invited me to join him for another round at the pub just across the street where, he said, there were some willing ladies. He was paying, so I agreed. Next thing you know I am whacked on the head and out cold. When I woke up I was lying on the deck of a Royal Navy ship already out at sea. Next to me were a dozen of the chaps I had been drinking with that night before. When my head cleared I protested my being impressed. The officer said I had agreed to join the navy and was given a shilling to secure the agreement. Henry said he thought about being uncooperative until he saw another one of the pressed sailors whipped for talking back to the midshipman. I figured I would get a bit of the same if I did not follow orders. I eventually volunteered my skills as a carpenter which must have made a big impression on the captain because in a few days I was officially designated a carpenter's mate. That got me a new uniform, a better bunk, and a box of carpenter's tools."

Henry had no choice but to make the best of a bad situation. He was stuck in the Royal Navy for five years. As the evening went on, Henry told several more stories from his Navy days. He said the age of press gangs pretty much ended but not entirely when it was outlawed. I remember reading about the impressment of Americans into the Royal Navy during the War of 1812. Starting in 1813 during the British naval blockade of the Chesapeake Bay, press gangs would attack American ships of all kinds in the bay, take able bodied men and press them into service in the Royal Navy. They also came ashore along the bay, the James River, the Potomac River, and the Rappahannock River to plunder the countryside and impress young men. Farmers tradesmen, teamsters, carpenters, and blacksmiths were taken against their will and made to serve in the Royal Navy. There is perhaps one positive side to the terrible practice of tearing men away from their homes and families by impressment. And that is the fact that more than 2000 enslaved African Americans in Virginia gained their freedom aboard British ships.

Henry said he had actually watched a man being keelhauled. He said it was horrible and the poor fellow was dead when they finally pulled him up. Henry said "the fellow was guilty no doubt about that, but what he did was hit an officer. Granted he deserved punishment but not to have his body torn apart as it was dragged over the barnacles on the hull. Henry said he saw a man flogged with 50 lashes for stealing cheese from the galley." Henry said the food wasn't bad when you were in port, but after a week at sea it got bad.

He said, "The hardtack biscuits were crawling with weevils, the salt pork was so salty it made your lips crack open and bleed, and the broth was so thin you could see through it to the bottom of the bowl."

Henry opined that he did not understand why they called British sailors Limeys. Then one day one of the mates explained that it was because the British Navy was the first to issue Limes to sailors to ward off scurvy.

One warm evening under a clear star filled night sky some of the sailors got to asking Henry questions about some of the expressions they had picked up. One asked where does the expression "cold enough to freeze the ball off a brass monkey" come from? Henry explained that when he was in the Royal Navy the ship carried hundreds of cannon balls. To conserve space the cannon balls were stacked in pyramid shaped stack on a base all called a brass monkey. On freezing cold days, as the story goes, the balls would contract and fall off the brass money. Thoroughly enjoying the storytelling, another sailor asked what the expression "Betwixt Wind and Water" means. Henry obliged the sailor by explaining that the area on a wooden ship's water line is exposed to both wind and water, depending on the weather, the wind, and the weight of the cargo. It is the ideal place to hit with a cannon ball if you are attempting to sink an enemy ship. It has come to mean a valuable spot. Yet another sailor asked Henry to explain the expression "Hand and fist." Henry described it as the act of climbing up and down a rope or hauling in or letting out a sail. It described fast movement or rapid progress. Another young seaman asked about the kinds of punishment he saw in the Royal Navy. Henry thought for a moment and said there were many, but the one that was almost as bad a keelhauling was called "Running the Gauntlet." Henry described it: The person being punished was forced to run between two lines of officers or mates who hit him with clubs, whips, the flat sides of their swords belts or anything that could inflict pain or draw blood. It was another one of those cruel and inhuman punishments the Royal Navy was accustomed to doing to sailors.

Henry was a man of many abilities. He was well-read, a skilled carpenter,, a great storyteller, a philosopher and a creator of some very beautiful knot art. He would take a piece of white line or hemp and tie it into intricate patterns. They ranged from a small ball-shaped knot called a monkey's fist to a Celtic knot. A monkey's fist is a perfect example of a self-defense weapon. It is a way of adding weight to a line so it can easily be thrown between ships or to shore. Monkey's fists can be made in various sizes, even as large as a cannon ball. While monkey's fists today are as small as marbles, they can still pack a heavy blow on the head. I found it remarkable that Henry's gnarled and weathered hand could create such intricate and beautiful works of art. Henry made several larger creations that could be used as a picture frame, a fancy table mat, a guard for a knife and all sorts of decorative things. He made what he called a Celtic knot and gave it to me as present. It was an intricate design that must have taken him many hours to complete. From his stories of being impressed, I learned that he had some horrifying experiences, but they did not seem to affect his affable personality. Many of the men I encountered in my years at sea had fascinating stories. From lawyers and doctors escaping bad marriages, men in trouble with the law, escapees from debtors' prison, or men just unhappy with their lives or searching for adventure, their stories were as varied as were their religions and nationalities.

21

ON A VOYAGE that had me concerned from the very start, we were making headway on the Persian Gulf enroute to the port of BANDAR-E ŠĀHPŪR. To our port side was Oman and the legendary pirate coast. I had read in a shipping journal about the infamous Wahhabis, a kind of orthodox Muslim group of people that dominated the southern part of the Persian Gulf. They organized raids on foreign ships at the behest of the vice-regent of the Pirate Coast, Husain bin Ali. The vice-regent allowed the Wahhabis to plunder all types of foreign ships, provided he received one-fifth of the proceeds for their piracy. Things got progressively worse starting in 1805. With military and financial backing from the Emirate of Dir'iyah, Qasimis aimed to spread Wahhabi doctrines across the Gulf region. Their naval force was powerful, and they used it to end the rising European colonial infiltration on their trade and commercial routes. Throughout the 1800s, the Wahhabi-Qasimi navy continually launched naval attacks on the British fleet and merchant ships. The British decided to hit the Sheikhs where they lived. In an effort to discourage the pirates, the British began bombarding the coast. In a short time, Ras Al Khaimah surrendered. The bombardment of other coastal settlements resulted in the Sheikhs of the coast agreeing to sign treaties of peace with the British. The British had a stunning victory that resulted in a number of preliminary agreements. They got the Sheikhs to agree to turn over land for the establishment of a British Garrison. Then came the <u>General Maritime Treaty of 1820</u>
. The wording, in part, was as follows. "There shall be a cessation of plunder and piracy by land and sea on the part of the Arabs, who are parties to this contract, forever." The stipulation was the Arabs must agree on land and sea, to carry a flag--a red rectangle contained within a white border of equal width to the contained rectangle. It could have either letters or no letters . The flag was to be a symbol of peace with the British government and with each other. The vessels of the "friendly Arabs" were to carry a paper (register), signed by their chief and detailing the vessel. They would also carry a documented port clearance that had to be presented on request to any British or other vessel which requested them. In essence it was a treaty of peace which also banned the slave trade. Many rumors had circulated that claimed the "friendly Arabs" were not always sticking to the agreement. There we were, sailing right smack into the middle of what were arguably the most dangerous pirate waters in the world.

The lookouts were doubled, and I ordered weapons to be stacked on the deck. The first few hours of sailing were delightful. There was a stiff breeze, and we were able to steer a straight course. Then the lookout shouted "Sail ho." There off our starboard bow was a sloop heading directly for us. The sailing master ordered more sail to increase our speed. The sloop was closing the gap between us rapidly. For a moment it appeared the sloop was going to sail right by us. Then the rudder on the sloop was turned hard to starboard, her sails slackened and she came about in a broad half circle which put her dangerously close to our course on our starboard quarter.

In a marvelous demonstration of seamanship, before we knew it, the sloop was alongside. Although there were several men on the deck, no armed men were visible. The captain shouted a heavily accented "Friendly," then waved a white flag and said that they he just wanted to trade. The crewman on the sloop threw a few grappling lines and we sailed in tandem. The mate circulated among the crew telling them to hold their fire, but keep their weapons at the ready. The captain came to the gunnel and made his intention to talk quite clear. He was an Arab, well dressed in his flowing robe and gutrah headpiece. A belt across his chest held a scabbard with a curved dagger. There were no gunmen visible on the sloop. I greeted the sloop captain, and he replied in remarkably good English. He said he wanted to trade and asked about our cargo. I did not explain our manifest. I asked him what he had to trade. He motioned to a crewman who brought forward two struggling women. One was rather comely and simply dressed, the other extremely well dressed and beautiful. Her eyes pleaded to me for help. Neither spoke any English.

The captain said he would trade the two "slaves" for cotton if we had any, and for grain. I concluded the women were not at all slaves but had been kidnapped, probably from a passing ship the "friendly" Arabs had attacked. I wanted to rescue the women, so I agreed to ten bales of cotton in exchange for the women. The deal was done without a shot fired and the ladies were made comfortable in my cabin. I directed the Mate to be sure they were fed and made to understand we mean no harm. The pirates sailed off with their cotton and we headed on to the port of BANDAR-E ŠĀHPŪR. I wondered just how to deal with our new passengers. We reached port the following afternoon. I signaled for a pilot who spoke no English but was quite impressed when the two ladies appeared on deck. The pilot did a good job of getting us in. Before long we were nestled nicely to a busy pier. The pilot bid us farewell and bowed a thank you. When the gangway was in place I made the ladies understand that I was going to take them ashore to the office of the East India Company, where they would be well taken care of, and find all the help they needed to return to their homes. My mates and I walked ahead to lead the way. No sooner did we exit the gangway than several armed and uniformed men grabbed us and took us prisoners. I tried to look back to see they were not mistreating the ladies and received a whack on the side of my head for my trouble. We were ungraciously thrown into what I assumed they called a jail. it was actually more like a very ripe and filthy pig stye. I demanded someone contact the East India Company.

My mate and I sat there chained to the wall and lying on dirty straw wondering what in the world had just happened. It took about four hours before a little man, quite well dressed arrived. He was dressed like a proper Englishman and did a lot of smiling and bowing. The guards who had been so rough with us when they arrested us, were now also bowing and scraping . They walked us over to the East India Company office where we were treated like heroes. We were offered food, wine, and a place to do our ablutions. Once we were cleaned up and ready to meet the bigwigs, we were escorted to a conference room where there were a dozen Arabs and one who seemed to be the head sheikh. He greeted me warmly and gave me a big hug.

We all sat down, and more refreshments were served, but there was no wine served. The Sheikh introduced himself as Abdul Mohamed Hassan, he spoke like an Englishman. He explained that he had been educated in London. Then he apologized for the misunderstanding and for our arrest. He said the ladies were his daughter and her companion who had been abducted by pirates some weeks before.

When the pilot advised the local police that the missing ladies were seen aboard my ship they assumed we were the ones who had abducted them. It was not until the ladies arrived at their home that he learned of their rescue. He said they were so excited to see them that the facts of our being the rescuers was not understood for a long period. The Sheikh said it was not until his daughter asked if my officers and I could be honored at a grand dinner, that he got the true story. He said that he would provide a separate party for my crew and that he would provide a security guard for the ship so that all could attend.

And it was a grand dinner indeed, held on the next evening. My mate and I had been transported back to ship. The next evening wearing our best uniforms, shaved and looking quite ready for a party, we were picked up by horse-drawn coaches and driven to the Sheikh's mansion. We all sat at a long table with the Sheikh at the head. Seated next to him was the young lady I had rescued who turned out to be his only daughter. I explained to the sheriff that I made the trade with the pirates because, having seen the women on the deck of the pirate's ship, I did not want to risk their getting hurt if a battle ensued. Again, he thanked me and gave me a big hug. The Sheikh asked several questions about England. He said some of his fondest memories were of his time at Oxford College. During summer vacation he had spent a great deal of time visiting London. He loved the Tower of London and Big Ben. We talked about the English countryside, and the history of England. He was very interested in America and said he hoped one day to visit.

After dinner we retired to a room where exotic desserts were served. It was there that I finally got a chance to talk to the young lady. Her name was Shaykhah Aliyah Hassan. Through an interpreter, I was able to speak with her. As we spoke I could not help but be taken with her beauty. She lived the very lavish lifestyle that the Sheikh provided for his entire family. She expressed her thanks. She too had many questions about America. I soon realized that she understood more English than I had realized. She seemed reluctant to try to speak English out of fear of getting it wrong. I encouraged her, under the watchful gaze of her nearby chaperone, to speak my language. She laughed and seemed to be having a genuinely good time. As a gift to show his gratitude, the Sheikh gave me a beautiful hand carved wooden chest. The edges had brass metal coverings. It had a top shelf with a dozen compartments filled with various spices and covered by little doors. Beneath the shelf there was a red velvet lined space. In it was a traditional curved Arabian dagger. It was in a gold scabbard trimmed with silver and inscribed with a message written in Arabic that he translated: "*To captain Patrick Sweeny, May you live a thousand years, my deepest gratitude for the heroic rescue of my daughter. You have my eternal gratitude, Sheikh Abdul Mohamed Hassan.* He also gave every one of my officers and crewmen a gold sovereign. In the following days I had a chance to speak with a gentleman form the East India Company. He explained the enormous wealth and power of the Sheikh. He introduced me to an admiral of the Royal Navy who questioned me about the pirate I had encountered. He vowed he would chase him down and bring him to justice and see him hung on the pier in the port. After we loaded cargo we sailed home accompanied by a Royal Naval frigate escort.

22

OUR ESCORT LEFT us at the entrance to the Strait of Ormuz as we headed toward the Gulf of Oman. It was smooth sailing on the Arabian sea as we made headway for a passage through the Suez Canal and home. Everything was in shipshape and Bristol fashion, we were on an even course running in a light chop. Then like a blast out of nowhere the wind whipped through the sails, the sky turned grey, and lightning sizzled across the darkening sky. The crew knew what to do and were ready for the command which came instantly from the sailing master. He shouted, "Trim sails". Crew men scrambled to set up lifelines and batten down the hatches and anything that might possibly move as the ship began to heave. Then the rain began hurtling down from the sky stinging the faces of all who dared look to the heavens for an explanation. Waves began to grow larger and larger and smash violently against the hull. We endured the pounding for a day, keeping the onslaught of angry seas to our bow with just a topsail. At dusk the topsail tore off. We turned and received a wave broadside that felt as if it would capsize the ship. Then in the dark of the blackest night, we took a wave astern. The cracking sound of the rudder being torn off echoed through the ship. Then there was a loud banging as it was slammed against the transom. Then quiet. All aboard save the cabin boys knew we had lost our rudder and were now completely at the mercy of the raging sea. The ship was in very real danger of being capsized by the merciless sea. Then as quickly as it had arrived, the cruel storm disappeared. The sky cleared and there we were drifting somewhere in the Indian ocean.

The following morning the lookout shouted a welcome "land ho!" The mate lowered the longboat and put a crew to towing our ship toward land. A light breeze came up and the mate jury-rigged a foresail which eased the work of the towing crew. I set to work finding out where we were. Obviously, the storm and the loss of our rudder had gotten us off course, I wanted to know just how far. I figured that we were in the Indian Sea approaching Seychelles, which is part of an archipelago of one hundred and fifteen Islands, of which Victoria is the capitol. By nightfall we had reached the entrance to the harbor and dropped anchor. In a short time, the harbor master arrived, and we told him our tale of woe. He assured us that everything we needed could be found in the port. Our carpenter headed for the lumber yard in search of wood suitable to make a new rudder. He also needed to find a blacksmith to make the fittings. Sychelles is very British; I felt quite at home visiting the local East India Company. In fact, I picked up some cargo of spices and coconuts. It is a beautiful island and amazingly developed for a place so far out in the sea. It took a week to get us ready for sea. Then refreshed and provisioned, we were on our way to Madagascar.

23

MADAGASCAR IS SOUTH of Seychelles at a distance of 1,112 nautical miles. With a good wind the trip should take about a month. Actually, we made it in a little less and entered the Bombetoka Bay Harbor with a very friendly English speaking pilot at the helm. There are several ports; we chose the major port of Mahajanga. The pilot was a kind of a self-appointed tourist guide for Madagascar in that he spent the time telling us about the country in glowing terms. And, from what we saw, he was not exaggerating. It was very beautiful. Once we finished the routine of docking, I went in search of the East India Company office. Things went easily there. And frankly it felt like home with everyone speaking and looking very British. Afterwards I spent some time browsing through the many shops along the main street. For a very isolated country, it had an incredible amount of goods from all over the world. Around dinner time I spotted a very Irish looking Pub called Mulligans. Once inside you would think you were in Ireland. I knew I was in an authentic Irish pub when I read the menu, which was headed by bangers and mash. It included Irish ham and cabbage and soda bread.

I sat down at a table and ordered a tankard of beer. When I looked around, low and behold, sitting at a table not far away was my old friend Sean Kelly, looking very handsome in his captain's uniform and now sporting a beard and mutton chops. The years and the beard threw me off a bit, but as soon as he spoke, I knew for certain that It truly my good friend of long ago. We hugged and laughed and shook hands. It was a grand reunion. We ate a wonderful Irish meal of Dublin Coddle made with seafood instead of the traditional sausages. It was served with lots of gravy and boiled potatoes that we washed down with plenty of Irish ale. The proprietor made the beer right there on the premises. Sean and I swapped sea stories until late in the evening. The next morning, we met again. It was like old times, strolling through the seaport window shopping, and chatting all the way. We found a Chinese restaurant and enjoyed a meal as we had so many years before. The only thing missing was the smiling face of the charming Mayling.

Queen Ranavalona, the ruler of Madagascar was not at all pleased with the British. She expelled British missionaries from the island and persecuted the remaining Christian converts. In 1854 Radama II, a Roman Catholic, secretly invited Napolean III to invade Madagascar. It was a desperate situation while we were there. The people at the East India Company advised us to make sail as soon as possible. Sean and I sailed our ships out of the bay the following morning. In time, France took control of Madagascar.

A day out of Madagascar a stowaway was discovered in among the cargo. At first the stowaway appeared to be a young boy but when brought to my quarters for interrogation, I soon discovered the stowaway was actually a very frightened young woman. Fortunately, she spoke English as well as French, so communicating was no problem. The problem was more related to a woman onboard a ship full of crewmen not all of whom were gentlemen. In my conversation with her I realized very quickly that she was no Judy. She was a well-educated young lady who had been through a terrible ordeal. I assigned her one of the passenger cabins . Since we did not have any passengers on this trip, she was afforded some privacy. But then I had to figure out what further precautions I had to take to prevent her being the brunt of any of my crews' ungentlemanly intentions. We were headed for Limerick, a voyage I estimated should take about two months with a fair wind. My stowaway took her meals with the officers and became a welcome guest. I noticed my officers were all of sudden clean shaven and assuming the manners that befit the presence of a lady. The use of profanity disappeared, and they were on their best behavior.

We learned that the young lady's name was Deloris Pennington and that she was the daughter of a Christian missionary couple that had been murdered by agents of Queen Ranavalona. Deloris had been in hiding since their murder, waiting to find an opportunity to stow away. The opportunity came when we were loading cargo that included sacks of nuts. Deloris bribed one of the men carrying the sacks, then she sewed herself into one of the sacks along with a quantity of beans. The stowaway suffered from mal di mare while hiding in the hold. As time when on, Deloris told us more of what Queen Ranavalona had done in her vengeance against Christians and her own son. The Queen for some reason had a terrible hatred for Christians She was obsessed with ridding her country of their presence and any vestiges of their missionary work.

I started calling Deloris Penn and the name stuck. It was during the telling of those sad stories that Penn often wept. The weather was good, and the seas were kind for our voyage back to Limerick. There was no trouble from the crew and eventually I gave her free roam of the decks. Penn loved to stand in the bow and allow the salt spray to dampen her clothing. She learned to climb up to the crows next and would stay for hours, which was a great treat for the lookout. Although she was very sophisticated for her 17 years, Penn was at heart, still a very curious and intelligent young girl. When she got her sea legs and her initial sea sickness ended, Penn embraced the life at sea. After a few weeks she mastered the use of the sextant, could read a compass and was beginning to learn how to plot a course on a chart. She took on duties without being asked. For example, she made it her job to brew and supply coffee to the helmsman on duty. She begged to be allowed to steer, and in smooth waters she often did just that. I saw Penn as myself at her age and I invited her to enjoy my books on navigation and the sea. One I recall she enjoyed reading was one of my favorites. It was titled *Frank Mildmay or The Naval Officer*, written by Captain Frederick Marryat. Penn got along quite well with the cabin boys. I would have thought there would have been a rivalry, but to the contrary, they seemed to see in her a friend, perhaps akin to a big sister. Penn learned to climb up the rigging to the crow's nest and in time knew the proper way to identify what she saw on the horizon. By then she had cut her hair and wore sailor clothes donated by various crew members. In a particularly nasty sea, a crewman accidently cut himself rather badly with his own knife. Penn was quick to help him and by the time I got to him she had the situation well in hand. Penn had stopped the bleeding and was cleaning the wound. She told me she thought he would need several stitches and I agreed. She said it was a clean would with a clean knife so she thought cleaning it with some whiskey might work, and that cauterizing would not be necessary. She sutured the wound, much to my amazement. Penn did a good job of bandaging the wound. At dinner that evening I complimented Penn on her medical skills and asked where she learned them. She explained that the mission her father ran was also a mini hospital where her dad and mom attended to the corporal as well as the spiritual needs of the natives who attended the mission. Penn said there was rivalry between her dad and the local witch doctors who strongly resented the usurping of their mumbo jumbo medicine by her parent's real medical skills.

I was delighted to have Penn as my unofficial medical assistant. She had complete access to my medical kit and soon became an avid reader of my Ship's Captain Medical Guide. Penn was comfortable treating a sunburn, boils, toothache, cuts, bruises, fever, and she could recognize a malingerer. Which she did often and with a charm and grace that had the complaining seaman apologizing for his weakness. Perhaps the most impressive thing that Penn did during her time on my ship was to hold a Sunday morning prayer service on the Poop deck. It started with a few of the cabin boys, then expanded until many of the crew, most of the officers and I attended regularly when the seas permitted. Penn would read the bible, recite some familiar prayers, and give a short sermon. Her father had taught her well.

When we reached Limerick two weeks later than planned, I immediately contacted the missionary group Penn had told me had sponsored her parents. They accepted Penn and assured me she would be well cared for and be an important part of their organization. It was a touching scene when the crew assembled to bid Penn farewell. Wearing a lovely dress the mission people had brought along for the occasion, Penn thanked the crew and me for our kindness to a poor bedraggled stowaway. Then she asked God's blessing for us all and wished us "Fair winds and following seas." All assembled shouted "Hip, hip Hooray" three times.

24

As time went on, I visited sweet Nora every time my ship returned to Limerick. We would go on picnics and visit historic places around Limerick. Her dad allowed me to use his horse and buggy each time I visited. Nora was particularly fond of visiting an old ruin called Carrigogunnell which means "Rock of the Candle." It got its name, according to local folklore, from a story about how the castle was occupied by a wizened hag who lit a candle every night. Anyone who looked at the candle would die before dawn. Wearing a magic cap, the local hero Regan broke the curse. There was not much of the old castle left but there was a window and as the sun set, it appeared as if there was a light in the window. Nora loved to watch the sun go down and strike the window until it glowed.

There were thirteen old castles around Limerick, and Nora and I visited every one. One of my favorites was King John's Castle in nearby Adare. On Sundays, if I was in port, we went to church together. Nora and her mom sang in the choir. I sat with her dad. Nora had a beautiful voice, and she often sang solo parts. I remember one time she sang Ave Maria and everyone in the cathedral was touched. Some were weeping. I must admit my eyes were close to flooding with tears. Her sweet soprano voice seemed to gain power as it echoed off the cathedral walls. I was brimming with pride as we exited the church after mass.

Before long I proposed, and she agreed that one day we would marry. But not before we got her father's consent. That was an adventure in itself. Nora instructed me on the correct procedure, and I followed it to the letter, dressed in my best captain's uniform and wearing my gold braid decorated cap. I arrived at the appointed hour to ask Nora's dad for her hand in marriage. She waited patiently while her dad, puffing on his pipe, asked me all the obligatory questions. I explained that I had ample funds to support Nora. That I was going to give up the sea. That I was going to buy a home in America in New York City. That I was planning to start a new business and that I had already picked out some horses to take home. The old man starting talking about Nora's dowery and the usual cash payment. I said I would require no dowery or cash payment. He said he would pay for the wedding. I told him I would pay for Nora's passage to America. Finally, we shook hands and Nora came in from the kitchen with a tray of drinks. Hugs and kisses followed from her mom and dad.

25

ON MY NEXT voyage we were sailing off the coast of Africa when we ran into a fierce storm that tore up our sails as we rounded the treacherous Cape of Good Hope. We lost our rudder, then hit the first of two reefs, then we smashed into the second. The ship came apart violently. I tried to save my sextant and the ship's log, but we were sinking so fast that I knew if I did not get out of my cabin, I would go down to Davy Jones's locker. I fought my way up the stars against a torrent of saltwater pouring into my cabin. I was holding the railing in one hand and trying to hold onto to a crystal decanter full of brandy, the only thing I managed to save besides my skin. I really did not have to jump overboard because the ship had by then sunk to where I just needed to walk off and swim away from the ship before it pulled me down. At first, I did not see anyone because the sea was rough, and the wind was howling. I grabbed a hatch cover that luckily, was floating nearby and hung onto it for dear life. A called out several times before I heard an ahoy from what turned out to be my first mate. We paddled with our hands toward each other, then he climbed aboard a precarious perch. Moments later one of the crew men floated near us. He was bleeding from a head wound, but held himself afloat by clinging to a barrel. The waves were about three feet high, so I could only see other survivors as the waves peaked. In a very short time the ship sank, and we were floating in the sea with all sorts of flotsam and jetsam and several wounded sailors around us. The mate and I gathered up as much of anything that would float and with some line we had pulled off a broken yard arm, we bound them all together into a makeshift raft. Slowly the float grew bigger and the number of men who managed to swim to it grew. By nightfall we had a decent size raft. Most of us just lay flat resting and wondering what would happen to us. By morning the seas had calmed, the wind died down and the sun warmed us from the cold of the night.

We drifted that way for two days. I offered my crew sips of the brandy from my decanter. I had tied it to a chunk of mast and kept it floating with us. Things were getting desperate. We had no food, no water, no sail, no mast, no oars, and no way to get them. The days dragged on, some of the men were considering drinking seawater. Then like an apparition out of the mist, two native catamaran boats appeared. They were paddling and drumming. Soon they made it clear they were there to rescue us. They had fruit which they passed to each of us and a wooden cask of water that we eagerly shared. They were African natives, all men, dressed in a kind of abbreviated shorts. Several had what appeared to be white ivory objects pierced into their ears and noses. Some wore necklaces made of animal teeth. I first thought they were human teeth; then I realized they were much larger than human teeth. At that point we did not care how they looked, we were just so grateful they had rescued us and brought us fruit and water. Once they got us all into their catamarans, they started paddling. Obviously, they knew where the land was, but we had no idea. It took nearly an hour to land on a beautiful white sandy beach. The shore was crowded with men, women, and children. The children were buck naked. The women were in colorful sarongs, similar to what I had seen women wearing in Hawaii. They were naked from the waist up.

They were excited to see us and were very helpful landing the boats and escorting the injured to their nearby village. One of the things that struck me as the native men started getting out of the boats was how tall they were. It was a short walk to the village. The huts were made of some kind of reed attached to bamboo poles. It struck me that they were not unlike the thatched roof buildings in Ireland that Dad had told me about. There were, however, no blocks, just more reeds. The floors of the huts were covered with a kind of reed mat. We rested in the huts for the remainder of the day and that night. By morning I was feeling better and ventured out of the hut.

The little village was very busy. There were women with children busy washing and doing what appeared to be routine household chores. The men were gathered around a larger hut.

Some were smoking a kind of pipe while others were busy working on spears made of bamboo. They were all very friendly and I did not feel at the least bit threatened. In fact, when the man I believed to be their leader saw me, he gestured to me to join him. We sat on reed mats in a small circle in front of his large hut. Judging by the numerous weapons spears and other weapons standing around the group, I pretty much got the idea that this was a warrior tribe. I thanked God they were friendly, at least so far. The chief was tall like the rest, but obviously older. His hair was gray and curly. He sat at the head of our group and attempted to communicate. Then we went into an impromptu hand gesture language and he made it clear to me that I was the guy in the boat that had sunk, and he was the rescuer, and he was happy he was able to help us. We chatted for a while then a young topless girl brought over what looked like a kind of banana but not quite the same. It had been roasted; actually it tasted quite good. I had noticed several long-horn cattle roaming around the village so I was sort of hoping the chief would invite me to dinner and that it would include meat. After a while I strolled back to the hut they had assigned me to check on my ship mates. Most were recovering nicely, but one of the two cabin boys seemed to be very ill. He was just a lad of twelve but a brave young man. He was hot with fever and his leg was turning black from what I believed to be gangrene. As the ship was sinking his leg had been crushed by a falling yard arm. One of the native women was trying to keep him cool and comfortable. They had put some kind of mushy poultice on his leg, but it did not help. Young Frederick Bannister died that evening. I was dreading having to face his family when and if we ever got back to England. He was a beautiful boy who might have one day been a brave man. We buried him in a field near the hut. The native women cried as we pounded a makeshift cross into the ground at the head of his grave. We rested in the native village for about a week. The chief offered to lead us to a man he called "Bwana." Then he assembled a group of about a dozen of his warriors, all armed with spears that were decorated with ribbons. They were mostly bare-chested with a kind of bandolier across their chests. On their waists they had leopard skins. Each wore a headdress that made it look as if they had strangely blonde hair. As we began our journey, many women wearing earrings and colorful sarongs gathered along the route. Some were quite attractive, while many of the others looked like men. Several had unusual haircuts that made them look as if their heads were very long and protruded from the rear. They did a lot of laughing and singing. We walked for a few hours, then the leader motioned for us to rest. Then after we all had a drink from an animal skin canteen, we traveled on until nearly dusk. Our escorts set up a camp and posted a lookout. Then they create a hearty soup with lots of vegetables and just a tiny bit of meat. Perhaps it was because we were all so hungry it tasted absolutely delicious. About midafternoon of the following day, we arrived at a large village where a crowd of men, women, and lots of children greeted us. A white man dressed in a white suit with a neatly dressed white woman at his side came forward. He was obviously a missionary. Both wore straw hats. He seemed as glad to see us as we were to see him. At last, I hoped, he was someone who spoke English.

We all shook hands and introduced ourselves. He was from London, as was his wife. They were part of an Anglican missionary group that had established a mission in the heart of Africa. He inquired about my persuasion and was disappointed to learn I was Catholic. I assured him most of my crew were Protestant. The crew were escorted to some nice huts while my first mate and I were invited to dine in the home of our hosts, the reverend August Martin Chambers and his wife Beatrice Marine. They offered us a hot cup of delicious Peking tea. I had not had a cup of tea in a dog's age. The couple wanted to hear where we were from, how we got to their village and any news we had from home. Then a very attractive girl called us in to dinner. The Reverend introduced her as his daughter Constance. The dinner was wonderful and pretty much the kind of cooking we were used to. Mrs. Chambers said she tried to adapt what food they could get there in Africa with typical English home cooking. She did, in fact, have it worked out pretty well and had trained their native woman cook to do a fine job. We rested there with the Chambers and our ship's cook found his way into their kitchen and was invited to prepare several meals while we were there.

After about two weeks with the Chambers and enjoying many evenings of conversation and pipe smoking together, it was time to move on toward civilization. The Reverend said that a mail boat stopped at the village about once a month and that the next one would be there in three days. I wanted to get word to Nora that I was OK, because I feared she would have heard that we were missing and assumed I had drowned. Right on time the mail boat arrived, and we boarded the trip to the nearest center of civilization, about three days' travel from Melbourne.

26

In Melbourne I managed to get a job as captain of a China Clipper. Her masters had died at sea and the first mate got her in to Melbourne. I was thrilled because I had always wanted to sail a clipper. They were beautiful and fast ships that beat all sorts of records in the China trade. *Lighting* was a beauty. She was 237 feet at the hull, 277 feet overall. Her beam was 44 feet. And she displaced 3,500 tons. She was a three masted full-rigged cargo clipper, she was clipper rigged and had a crew of 100. Her main mast was 164 feet above the deck. She carried 13,000 yards of canvas under all plain sail. Her home port was Liverpool. I was pretty familiar with sailing a clipper. Several years before, I had served as mate on one for about a year.

With the help of my first mate, Mr. Archibald Harrington III, who was born in Dublin and went to sea as a boy as I did, I settled very quickly into my new command. Archie had been mate on the *Lighting* for ten years, ever since she was built. He was a grand chap. We became good friends and enjoyed many a night in my cabin swapping yarns about our lives and the sea. I guess I talked a lot about Nora, as he did about his love, Fiona.

He told me how he had been arrested in Canton one time because he thought he was being cheated in a restaurant. It turned out he was, and he was released with an apology in time to sail with his ship. I related the story about how I was arrested in Liverpool. One night after my ship was loaded and ready to sail on the morning tide, I was strolling along the dock, just enjoying a walk and checking over the ship. As I approached the stern there were two bobbies sitting on the bulkhead, having a wonderful time. They were making fun of the American flag hung from the transom of our ship. They may have been drinking. I know I was. As I approached, they called me "Yank" and told me I should take my rotten old ship with its rotten old flag back to America because it was stinking up the neighborhood. I was furious and I picked up a board I found lying on the dock and began to beat the devil out of both. They fought back while frantically blowing their whistles. A wagon full of bobbies arrived and whacked me a few times with their clubs They put me in a "paddy wagon."

I spent the night in jail, then I was surprised to be released early the next morning and escorted back to my ship. The bobbies said I was being released because the ship's agent paid my bail and because the ship could not sail without a captain. He said further that I could never get off the ship in Liverpool. I was banned for life. I never liked Liverpool anyway. In retrospect that incident was humbling and a great embarrassment to me. I always knew I had a temper and truly strived to keep it under control. Unfortunately, I came to the realization that my ability to control my temper was weakened considerably when I consumed too much alcohol. All of my life, It has been a struggle for me to keep demon rum from getting the best of me.

One of the great joys of my life is the marvels I have seen during my many voyages to enchanting places around the world, including the beauty of Rome, the miracle of Venice, the dykes of Holland, the majesty of the Alps, the serenity of China, the mysticism of India, the royal heritage of London, the rugged beauty of Ireland, and the Suez Canal. I traversed the Suez Canal soon after it was nearly completed and opened for traffic. The idea of building a canal goes back centuries. It finally happened in 1869. The Suez Canal stretches 120 miles from Port Said on the Mediterranean Sea in Egypt southward to the city of Suez. It separates the bulk of Egypt from the Sinai Peninsula. The canal took ten years to build and cuts through the Isthmus of Suez, a stark and barren land with stifling heat. Our ship had to be towed through the canal, and during that slow trip I could not help but try to imagine what it must have been like for the builder, the French engineer, Ferdinand de Lesseps.

. It took him years to cut through from the Red Sea to the Mediterranean, a distance of over 120 miles. There are no locks. The area includes some lakes, but mostly is a straight man-made canal through the Isthmus. It is mind boggling to imagine the work it took to dig it out. The toll in human suffering must have been enormous for the 30,000 workers who actually did the digging.

27

O**N ANOTHER VOYAGE** I recall, we sailed out of London with a cargo of farm tools, wagons, ten draft horses and about a dozen passengers, mostly French and a few Chinese. We were headed for Tahiti and the of Port of Papeete. Some of the passengers said they were doing business with a great plantation at Atimaono. One of the passengers, a British professor of naval history from Oxford University, Sir Reginal Blake, said he was hoping to find some old church records and possibly some descendants of British people who lived in Tahiti. It all started when he was browsing through some old magazines in the Oxford Library and he came upon an article in *The Gentlemen's Quarterly* from 1790. It contained a fascinating story of a brutal captain, a mutinous crew and survival. The actual story occurred in the same waters we were traveling, Blake said. The *HMS Bounty* departed England on December 23, 1787 headed for Tahiti. The mission was to collect a cargo of breadfruit saplings to transport to the West Indies. There, the breadfruit would serve as food for enslaved passengers. Things were going well until the ship neared Cape Horn in March. The weather turned atrocious, with wave after wave battering the ship. I could identify with the professor's story, because I had also battled Cape Horn in winter. Sir Reginal was very interested in my battles with Cape Horn. Captain Bligh had no choice but to steer the *Bounty* on a 10,000-mile detour past Africa and Australia. Aside from the unfortunate weather, it seemed like a normal voyage until the ship reached Tasmania's Adventure Bay in late August. Captain Bligh was an incredibly mean man, stuck in the old ways of brutal punishments for his crew. As the story goes, Bligh had words with the ship's carpenter, William Purcell. Purcell was well liked by the crew. Unjustified criticism by the captain stirred their resentment. Purcell did not take the reprimand well and accused the captain of nitpicking his work. Then death struck the ship. It happened in Tasmania, when a seaman, James Valentine, became infected after being bled by the surgeon, Thomas Huggan. Bligh blamed Huggan and the officers for this, but in the end, all that could be done was to continue to Tahiti. Resentment among the crew grew stronger and stronger.

The ship finally reached Tahiti after ten months at sea. It remained there for five months while the gathering of breadfruit saplings proceeded. The crew enjoyed an idyllic life. The climate was warm and comfortable. And the natives, especially the women, were extremely hospitable. Acting -Lieutenant Fletcher Christian fell in love with a Tahitian woman named Mauatua. With its mission completed, the *Bounty* departed Tahiti on April 4, 1789. The decks were packed with breadfruit saplings. Then on

April 28, near the island of Tonga, Christian and 25 petty officers and seamen seized the ship. Bligh, who eventually would fall prey to a total of three mutinies in his career, was an oppressive commander and insulted those under him. By setting him adrift in an overcrowded 23-foot-long boat in the middle of the Pacific, Christian and his conspirators had apparently handed him a death sentence. By remarkable seamanship, however, Bligh and his men reached Timor in the East Indies on June 14, 1789, after a voyage of about 3,600 miles. Bligh returned to England and soon sailed again to Tahiti, from where he successfully transported breadfruit trees to the West Indies.

The story captured my imagination to the point where I looked forward to dinner each evening to hear more of Professor Blake's account. The professor was a wonderful storyteller and described what happened with Fletcher Christian and the men who had taken over the *Bounty*. Christian and his men attempted to establish themselves on the island of Tubuai. Things did not work out there, so the *Bounty* sailed north to Tahiti, and 16 crewmen decided to stay there, despite the risk of capture by British authorities. Fearful they would be captured and sent back to England, Christian and eight others, together with six Tahitian men, a dozen Tahitian women, and a child, decided to search the South Pacific for a safe haven. They searched for a place where they hoped they would never be found. In January of 1790, the *Bounty* settled on Pitcairn Island, an isolated and uninhabited volcanic island more than 1,000 miles east of Tahiti. The mutineers who remained in Tahiti were captured and taken back to England where three were hanged.

28

THERE WAS ANOTHER time I wound up in the drink and pretty close to ending up in Davey Jones's locker, as sailors refer to drowning. I was still a cabin boy when we were blown off course by one of those sudden ferocious storms we often encounter at sea. Our sails were badly damaged, and the rudder torn off completely. We drifted along for a few days and saw land. It was a tiny speck of an island the mate showed me on our chart as Laccadive island. We had sailed around the Cape of Comorin at the south tip of India having left Ceylon with a cargo of tea, spices and tobacco. We were grateful to be drifting northward and toward the port of Mumbai. According to a book the mate had, there was an office of the East India Company located there. The following day the captain warned us we were drifting toward a reef off the coast of Maharashtra. The longboat was launched, and the crew frantically tried to change our course by towing the ship. They were having some success when another sudden storm defeated their effort. The longboat capsized, but our crew was able to get themselves back to the ship by hanging onto the tow line despite the waves and wind that were pushing the ship. The crew lowered the cargo nets midship and the battered crew of the long boat scampered back aboard. They sent me to the galley for hot broth for the men. I brought some coffee for the captain and the first mate as well. The longboat was trailing behind us when the ship hit a reef. In a matter of minutes we started to break up, Some of the men swam out to the longboat and were able to right it. Fortunately, the previous crew had secured the oars so the present crew could row.

The crew kept rowing the long boat away from the reef. Fortunately, maybe because I was praying so hard, the weather improved, and the seas calmed. They were able to keep the boat clear so that the survivors could swim to it. Miraculously, all souls aboard were saved. Some clung to the longboat, others floated on wood from the wrecked Ship. A few were lucky enough to hang on to empty barrels. One crewman hung onto a mattress and the tow line as the crew rowed toward what the captain said would be land. After about a day we spotted a sail which turned out to be a rescue ship of His Majesty's Indian Navy.

When we finally got aboard the rescue ship, we assumed would be manned by British sailors, we were surprised to find it crewed and captained by Indians. The captain spoke fluent English with a pronounced British accent. He said he was a graduate of the Royal Naval Academy in Portsmouth, England. The captain could not have been more gracious. After a hearty meal, our crew was assigned to a naval barracks with showers. Our captain was invited to stay at the rescue captain's home while in Mumbai. The following day our captain inquired about what ship might be landing in the next few days. He learned that there were some sixty ships at anchor and that one of the captains was very ill and in the local hospital. Our captain visited the East India Company office. The manager at the office said he was pretty sure that the ship would need a new captain, and very possibly might also need another crew. The ship had arrived with the captain already ill, offloaded their cargo and had been at anchor for a month. Most of the crew had found berths on other ships.

Liam, the third mate, and I took advantage of the time ashore visiting Mumbai. I had accumulated several coins in my ditty bag and was eager for another one of those Chinese meals. We spent much of the day visiting different shops, many with beautiful cotton clothing: vivid red, yellow, and rose colored dresses with gold thread embroidery. There were veils, almost transparent. For lunch we were grateful to have found a Chinese restaurant. It was very similar to the Chinese restaurant where we had met Mayling, but here the menus were in Chinese. It had the familiar aroma of incense I remembered from Mayling's place. Over dinner I told the story about how we had met Mayling. The mate teased me about having a crush on her. I assured him it was Sean that had the crush. I tried to impress him with my use of chopsticks, but it was soon apparent that he knew well how to use them. Then we talked about dinner. For dinner we planned try out Indian food. Imagine! We were talking about dinner while still eating lunch. I guess that came from being in the longboat without food.

We shopped for the rest of the afternoon, then found what looked like a nice restaurant. We entered a very lavishly decorated Indian restaurant with a strong aroma of spices, like we sometimes had in the cargo hold. Actually, I found out later it is called Garam masala, a common spice blend used in Indian cooking, that typically contains a mixture of spices such as cumin, coriander, cinnamon, cloves, and cardamom. The very nice middle-aged waitress spoke reasonably good English. She said her husband was the chef and they owned the restaurant. She told us that in Southern India rice is the staple food, and it is eaten with sambhar (sambar), a watery stew made of lentils, tamarind, and vegetables. We had that along with some pickled fruits and vegetables. They had a sample tray, so we ordered it to try some of the typical food. The tray came with portions of what was listed on the English version menu as Andhra, Tamil, Chettinad, Kerala and Mangalore, among others. Each region cooks sambhar differently and uses different varieties of rice. Tamil cuisine classifies food into six tastes—sweet, sour, salty, bitter, pungent, and astringent. They used a lot of curry and sometimes hot spices. Most of the portions that did not come in bowls were laid out on banana leaves.

Our visit to Mumbai was delightful and I got to know the third mate much better. Liam wasn't much older than me and he came from Ireland. Late that afternoon, loaded with the treasure we bought, we headed back to our new ship. Riding in the launch to the ship, I noticed the water was more brown than blue. It seemed to be very polluted.

Our new ship, *American Rover*, was loaded with cloth, indigo, sugar, and raw cotton bound for England. Liam thought there might be some opium onboard, but I never saw it, nor did he. After our disastrous shipwreck, the trip home was uneventful.

29

THERE WAS ANOTHER time I wound up in the drink and pretty close to ending up in Davey Jones' locker, as the sailors refer to drowning. I was still a cabin boy when we were blown off course by one of those sudden ferocious storms we often encounter at sea. Our sails were badly damaged, and the rudder torn off completely. We drifted along for a few days and saw land. It was a tiny spec of an island the mate showed me on our chart as Laccadive Island. We had sailed around the Cape Comorin at the south tip of India having left Ceylon with a cargo of tea, spices and tobacco. We were grateful to be drifting northward and toward the port of Mumbai. According to a book the mate had, there was an office of the East India Company located there. The following day the captain warned us we were drifting toward a reef off the coast of Maharashtra. The longboat was launched, and the crew frantically tried to change our course by towing the ship. They were having some success when another sudden storm defeated their effort. The longboat capsized but our crew was able to get themselves back to the ship by hanging onto the tow line despite the waves and wind that were propelling the ship. The crew lowered the cargo nets midship and the battered crew of the long boat scampered back aboard. They sent me to the galley for hot broth for the men. I brought some coffee for the captain and the first mate as well. The longboat was trailing behind us when our ship hit the reef. In a matter of minutes, it started to break up on the reef. Some of the men swam out to the long boat and where able to right it. Fortunately, the previous crew had secured the oars so the present crew could row.

The crew kept rowing the long boat away from the reef. Fortunately, maybe because I was praying so hard, the weather improved, the seas calmed, and they were able to keep the boat clear so that the survivors could swim to it. Miraculously, all souls aboard were saved. Some clung to the longboat, others floated on wood from our wrecked Ship. A few were lucky enough to hang on to empty barrels. One crewman hung onto a mattress and the tow line as the crew rowed toward what the captain said would be land. After about a day we spotted a sail which turned out to be a rescue ship of the His Majesty's Indian Navy.

When we finally got aboard the rescue ship we assumed would be manned by British sailors, we were surprised to find that crew and captain were Indians. The captain spoke fluent English with a pronounced British accent. He said he was a graduate of the Royal Naval Academy in Portsmouth, England.' The captain could not have been more gracious. After a hearty meal, the crew was assigned to a naval barracks with showers. Our captain was invited to stay at the rescue ship's captain's home while in Mumbai . The following day our captain inquired about what ship might be landing in the next few days. He learned that there were some sixty ships at anchor and that one of the captains was very ill and in the local hospital. Our captain visited the East India Company office. The manager at the office said he was pretty sure that the ship would need a new captain and very possibly might also need another crew. The ship had arrived with the captain already ill, offloaded their cargo and had been at anchor for a month. Most of the crew had found berths on other ships.

Liam, the third mate, and I took advantage of the time ashore visiting Mumbai. I had accumulated several coins in my ditty bag and was eager for another one of those Chinese meals. We spent a lot of the day visiting different shops. There were lots and lots of beautiful cotton clothing. The dresses had a lot of gold thread embroidery on some very vivid red, yellow, and rose-colored fabrics. There were also lots of veils that you could see through, almost transparent. For lunch we were grateful to find a Chinese restaurant in Mumbai. It was very similar to the Chinese to the Chinese restaurant where we had met Mayling. This was different: the menus were in Chinese. It had the familiar aroma of incense I remembered from Mayling's place. Over dinner I told the story about how we met Mayling. The mate teased me about having crush on her. I assured him it was Sean that had the crush. I tried to impress him with my use of chopsticks, but soon observed that he knew very well how to use them. Then we talked about dinner. For dinner we planned try out Indian food. Imagine! We were talking about dinner while still eating lunch. In the longboat, we had been too long without food.

We shopped the rest of the afternoon, then found what looked like a nice restaurant. As we entered the very lavishly decorated Indian restaurant, we sensed the strong aroma of spices, like the boxes of spices we sometimes had in the cargo hold. I found out later it is called Garam masala, a common spice blend in Indian cooking. Typically, it contains a mixture of spices such as cumin, coriander, cinnamon, cloves, and cardamom. The very nice middle-aged waitress spoken reasonably good English. She said her husband was the chef and they owned the restaurant. She told us that in Southern India rice is the staple food, and it is eaten with sambhar (sambar), a watery stew made of lentils, tamarind, and vegetables. We had that along with some pickled fruits and vegetables. They had a sampler tray, so we ordered it to try some of the typical food. The tray came with tastings from Andhra, Tamil, Chettinad, Kerala and Mangalore, listed among others on the English version menu. Each region cooks sambhar differently and uses different varieties of rice. Tamil cuisine classifies food into six tastes—sweet, sour, salty, bitter, pungent, and astringent— the cuisines used a lot of curry and sometimes very hot spices. Most of the portions that did not come in bowls were laid out on banana leaves.

On our delightful visit to Mumbai I got to know the third mate much better. Liam wasn't much older than me and came from Ireland. Late that afternoon, loaded with the treasure we bought, we headed back to our new ship. As we rode in the launch to our new ship, the water was more brown than blue. It seemed to be very polluted.

Our new ship the *American Rover* was loaded with cloth, indigo, sugar, and raw cotton bound for England. Liam thought there might be some opium onboard, but I never saw it, nor did he.

Compared to our having been shipwrecked, the trip home was uneventful.

On another voyage which took us to North Africa, we were sailing along the Barbary Coast when the lookout shouted "Sail ho! I didn't wait for the captain to order me; I ran for the glass and had it in his hands before he even got to call for it. He gave me a smile and immediately stretched it out and put it to his eye. I stood on the deck waiting for the captain's next command. Liam had told me there were many rumors and true stories about the Muslim pirates that roamed the waters of the Barbary Coast.

The lookout shouted that the ship had veered toward us and was making sped to overtake us. The captain ordered more sail, but in a short time the pirates' ship was nearly upon us. The captain ordered a white flag hoisted to main sail. Liam and I were surprised that the captain would give up the ship without a fight. Then I got the word whispered to me that the lookout had spied what he recognized as an American Naval, probably a sloop, making way toward us. The captain ordered the mate to get the ship's crew to battle stations without any noise. He told them to whisper all commands and keep their heads down on deck lest the enemy hear them. We did not have any cannons, but we were able to supply the crew with lots of rifles. The captain and the officers had pistols. On the front deck we had a funny looking gun called a blunderbuss mounted to the stern poop deck rail. Liam said when that gun was fired it spread chunks of metal over a broad area. It had a short barrel and a large bore. The end of it looked like a trumpet. When the pirate's smaller but faster ship got to within about 100 feet, the captain ordered the blunderbuss to be fired. I soon learned that it was not music coming out of that trumpet, it was hot metal. The lookout was still watching for the very large naval sloop that was making way rapidly and seemed to be unnoticed by the pirates. The pirates got midships of us and had men up in the rigging preparing to throw their grappling hooks and board us. A few shots rang out from their rigging but just tore holes in the wood of our deck. The captain ordered the crew to shoot. There was a loud bang. We did not feel it in the ship, which seemed strange. We thought the pirates had fired a broadside. In moments, they stopped shooting as their ship began to keel over to her port side. It turned out the navy sloop was midship of the pirate ship and fired a broadside into her below the water line. The pirate ship was sinking. In a short time, she was gone, leaving pirates flailing around in the water and clinging to some of the wreckage from their ship. Some of the crew fired at them, but our captain ordered them to stop. He said the navy would take care of them and put them in jail ashore. Safe again and after we thanked the captain of the U.S. Navy sloop, we made way for Greece. Later, over the next few days, Liam had read that not long ago some four thousand Christian slaves were rescued from the pirates by British and Dutch naval forces. Many were probably sailors just like us. He told me the pirates were essentially sponsored by the Arab rulers of Morocco, Algiers, Tunis, and Tripoli. Over the years many countries including the United States, had sent their navies and marines to get rid of the pirates. We never learned who the pirates were, but we kept a careful watch for the rest of the trip.

We entered the port of Piraeus, the ancient port of Athens with a Greek pilot at the helm. I was amazed to watch the captain, who took over the helm when we neared the dock. He steered the ship and took it down just enough for us to slowly glide into the dock. He also used an anchor thrown at just the right moment, held the bow and allowed the stern to swing into the dock. The crew got right to work offloading our cargo of spices, cotton, tools and just about anything you could imagine. The Greeks are a very sophisticated people with tastes developed over centuries. I was eager to explore the city but, the mate warned me to wait for the captain to say, "Well young man would you like to see the one of the world's oldest countries?" I answered in the affirmative and ran for the boarding ramp.

The port of Piraeus is just five miles from the city of Athens. It dates back to the fifth century BC and it is home to the largest naval base in all of Greece. It is a busy place packed full of shipping offices, warehouses, banks, shipyards, and many other secondary businesses such as shops and brothels. We hired a tour guide and hopped aboard his horse-drawn surrey. He was a charming fellow who spoke English quite well. He explained the sights of interest from the start of the tour. Our guide pointed out the remains of what were ship sheds. He explained that in ancient times ship sheds were a necessity for any sizeable fleet of ships, especially trireme Greek warships. These wooden vessels could not remain in the water indefinitely, so to prevent their becoming water-logged, damaged by weather extremes, encrusted with barnacles, and eaten by shipworms, they had to be pulled ashore and protected from the elements. Ship sheds were usually long narrow buildings (40 meters long by 6 meters wide) with a roof and open at the sea end. To provide good ventilation, their walls, rather than being solid, were often made only of pillars. There were hundreds of ship sheds in Piraeus at its peak. They were built on the limestone bedrock with a 1:10 incline to allow the ships to be pulled up, probably manually, stern first. Light maintenance work, such as coating the hull with anti-fouling paint, traces of which remain at the site. was also done in the sheds.

In a short time, we arrived at Hadrian's arch, built in the second century. From there we could see the Parthenon perched high up on a hill. Our guide told us to follow him as we walked through the gigantic remains of the Parthenon. He explained that it was built in thanksgiving for the Hellenic victory over Persian Empire invaders during the Greco-Persian Wars. Like most Greek temples, the Parthenon also served as the city treasury. Construction started in 447 BC when the Delian League was at the peak of its power. It was completed in 438; work on the decoration continued until 432. For a time, it served as the treasury of the Delian League, which later became the Athenian Empire. In the final decade of the 6th century AD, the Parthenon was converted into a Christian church dedicated to the Virgin Mary. After the Ottoman conquest in the mid-fifteenth century, it became a mosque. In the Morean War, a Venetian bomb landed on the Parthenon, which the Ottomans had used as a munitions dump during the 1687 siege of Acropolis. The resulting explosion severely damaged the Parthenon. From 1800 to 1803, the 7th Earl of Elgin took down some of the surviving sculptures, now known as the Elgin Marbles. That seemed like grave robbing to me. The guide let us know that he was not at all fond of what the earl had done. Fortunately, the guide had brought along some drink he kept in a cool well insulated case.

Our next stop was the Acropolis,. Our guide explained the Acropolis of Athens is an ancient citadel located on a rocky outcrop above the city of Athens and contains the remains of several ancient buildings of great architectural and historical significance, the most famous being the Parthenon He said the term acropolis is generic and there are many other acropoleis in Greece.

After walking in so much heat, it was a great relief to enter the Acropolis Museum. Just getting out of the sun was great, as were the not so cool drinks we were able to get there.

It was near sundown by the time the guide got us back to the port. We gave him a nice tip. His tour was informative and enjoyable. Before we parted he recommended a restaurant just down the street. We took him up on the recommendation and visited a small restaurant which, in addition to the food, featured a belly dancer. Neither of us had ever seen a belly dancer before and we were eager to see what belly dancing was all about. We suggested the waiter order for us and we settled back to enjoy the show. There were drums and what looked like a guitar and a fellow playing a kind of saxophone. The dancer appeared wearing bells, veils, a top and brief shorts which allowed her navel to show beneath the veils. Did a lot of turns and wiggles. Then she placed six coins on her abdomen and made them flip over without touching them. That to me was amazing. Then when the dance was finished she came over to the table and some of the men rolled up paper money, held it in their mouths and stuffed it into her cleavage. Others stuffed the bill into the top of her shorts, I think I must have been blushing because she patted me on the head and the audience laughed. The dinner was great, lots of pita bread, olives, hummus, feta cheese, salad, and several other great specialties I could not pronounce. I truly enjoyed the day and the conversation with the mates. Two days later we left Greece and were back to a work, sailing.

31

THE PORT OF Shimoda, Japan had only been open for a few years when our ship landed there. I was still a cabin boy, but I had become friends with one of the mates. He told me that Japanese ports had been closed to foreigners for two centuries. It seems the Japanese got tired of missionaries trying to convert the whole country to Christianity, so they threw them all out and allowed no one to land a ship in their country. Admiral Perry somehow convinced the Japanese to open the ports, perhaps because the British were forcing China to open its ports. For Japan, it turned out to be a game changer that rapidly embraced western technology and trade. In a short time, it led to the overthrow of the ruling shogun. The new ruler was an emperor who modernized the country.

We anchored in the harbor and used our longboat to transport goods. Then the mate and I toured the city, much cleaner than any port I had ever been in. We traveled by rickshaw, essentially a little Hansom cab pulled by a man instead of a horse. The shop owners did a lot of bowing and spoke pidgin English. It was a little tricky trying to buy anything, but we worked it out. They had graceful fans, strange shoes for ladies, and beautiful Kimonos. My friend had learned how to bargain the prices down. His trick was to shake his head when he heard the price and head for the door. Most of the time the storekeeper would call him back and offer a lower price.

For lunch we bought sushi from a little shop near the docks. It was made of rice with some kind of green dried leaves and seafood in the middle—delicious! They offered us sake but we had tea instead. Near the port was a beautiful garden with ponds and bridges. The little shelters in the garden had ornate roofs painted red and gold. The gardens were wonderfully manicured and meticulously plotted, with nothing growing wild. A shop near the entrance displayed small bonsai trees. Everything in Japan seemed to be very delicate. There were lots of hand carved vases and statues. Bowls, some beautifully hand painted, came in every size imaginable. It was the buildings themselves that struck me. They seemed to be made of paper stretched over bamboo, all with sliding doors. We looked in the window of a shop that was a pharmacy. It had some of the weirdest stuff I had ever seen: dried jellyfish, sea cucumbers, dried shrimp and stuff that looked like black dried seaweed. Dozens and dozens of jars contained who knows what--the labels were all in Japanese. None of it looked like I would ever want to take it, no matter how sick I might have been.

Walking through the city, we noticed that the women took tiny steps, like their feet hurt. The men walked just like we did. Many women carried umbrellas, even though it wasn't raining. The city was very busy with stuff being moved all over the place. It struck me as strange that I didn't see any horse drawn wagons like we used at home. Here, men did the work of beasts.

We had the opportunity to learn about the Geisha girls of Japan when we attended a geisha show and dinner. The Geishas are a class of performing artists, like ballet dancers. They are intensively trained to perform traditional Japanese performing arts. They are schooled in dancing, music and singing and they are trained to be good conversationalists. If you want to have a Japanese party, the geisha is the one to get to host. Geisha clothing is especially beautiful. The women wear beautiful kimonos and do their long trailing hair in a traditional style. Perhaps their most striking feature is the all-white facial makeup called *Oshiro*. Geishas will entertain at party called *Oza Shiki*. Having a party hosted by a Geisha is expensive, so it is generally done by wealthy clientele. Geishas will also perform on stage and at festivals accompanied by a kind of guitar music and singing that is totally alien to our idea of music. Many people assume the geishas are prostitutes. That assumption is quite understandable when you learn their history. Though in the past the ceremony of *mizauage*--the loss of a *maiko*'s virginity to a paying patron--took place historically as part of the transition from apprentice to geisha, nowadays the geisha are not prostitutes. Nevertheless, there may still be some who practice the older form. Japan was a fascinating place and incredibly different from than America. We had to get back to the ship; it was to sail on the morning tide.

32

I N MY EXPERIENCE sailors aboard a sailing vessel are in general a very mixed breed of men. Some are of the lowest caliber who could easily be in prison or had been many times. Those are hard drinking, filthy mouthed ruffians who would as soon slit your throat over a glass of beer as take an insult. Then there are the men who have gone to sea for the adventure. They might have been clerks, laborers or college professors who were fed up with their lives and looking to escape boredom or a failed marriage. There are some African crewmen whose skin is decorated with tattoos or scarred by whip or cut in a design by some tribal ritual. Their stories are as varied as the shells on a beach.

There are good captains and bad captains. Cruel captains and kind captains. The mates fall into the same categories. When they are good, life onboard is marvelous. When they are bad it is hell on earth. Then too, there are competent captains and the incompetent. A competent captain could possibly save the ship and your life with his expertise. An incompetent captain might easily run the ship aground or allow her to be capsized in a storm with all souls lost, including you.

I was fortunate to have mostly very good captains and crews that I respected. They were men that knew the sea and respected it. And they were willing to share their knowledge without the often-cruel lessons imposed by lesser men.

33

From Melbourne, we sailed my new ship *Lighting* to Canton and then up the Pearl River. We made 14 knots with a good wind and calm water. She was a dream to handle. The crew was seasoned and very good. They responded to sail changes wonderfully well and on the whole, they were a decent group of men. There was a towheaded cabin boy who came aboard that reminded me of myself at his age. He was eager and tried to act like a man, but somehow the young boy always showed through. One day I reprimanded him for dropping a tray and he cried. I felt terrible but I knew he had to learn to survive.

We took on a pilot and entered Canton harbor to offload our cargo of sugar, spices, indigo, cotton and rum. With the aid of the pilot, we sailed up the Pearl River Delta, South China's trading ports. The Pearl River, the third longest river in China, flows into the South China Sea through the southern Chinese province of Guangdong. The estuary of the river, called the Bocca Tigris, allows easy access by seagoing vessels.

Our cargo consisted of barrels of tin ore. Tin was used to strengthen bronze. We took on a cargo of porcelain packed in barrels and other decoration and furniture for the home. In addition, we carried bronze statues and bells. We made a stop in Spain where we offloaded and took on some new cargo. That gave me time to explore. I had heard of the famous bullfights in Cordoba, Spain, so I traveled there to see what all the excitement was about. There were several matadors, but the main attraction was Rafael Molina, "Lagartijo." I admired the bravery of the picadors and the matadors but I did not like the idea of killing a bull. As a kid growing up back on our farm in Ohio I dealt with a lot of cows, and grew fond of many. They had a warm personality of their own and if you worked with them for a while, you understood their emotions. We had an old bull who kept our cows freshed, but that's about all. He did not snarl and beat the ground like the bulls in the arena. The main event featured Rafael Molina "Lagartijo." He was from Cordoba and was famous for lying down in front of the bull and other gestures that ended up getting the officials to criticize his performance. The spectacle was bloody and cruel, yet at the same time there was a certain majesty to it all. Crowds loved every minute of it. The costumes, the music and the spectators intrigued me. Some of the women, especially those in the boxes down front, were beautiful. Most women wore a lace head covering that I found very attractive. But on the whole, I did not want to ever see another bull fight. I had seen enough cruelty of mean captains in the course of my life to try to avoid as much of it as I could.

I had the opportunity to visit the shops in Madrid. There were some really beautiful things. I wanted to bring a gift home to Nora, and I must have visited a dozen ladies' shops. I consulted one of the salespeople in a shop and she suggested I buy a mantilla. She showed me several, which I recognized having seen at the bull fight. She explained that a *mantilla* is a traditional Spanish and Latin American head covering and shawl made of liturgical lace or silk, Sometimes it is worn over a high comb called a *peineta*. I bought three different mantillas and three combs for Nora. Then I spotted a beautiful jewelry box lined with red velvet that I thought would go well for her jewelry. In another shop I bought a string of pearls and a brooch.

34

WE SAILED FOR Limerick laden with new cargo from Spain. We had fair winds and calm seas and made the passage in record time. By the time I reached Limerick, Nora had learned that I had survived. She was waiting for us at the dock. It was a grand reunion with lots of hugs and kisses. Once the ship was secured in the hands of Mr. Huntington, I traveled to Nora's home. There was a lavish dinner with lots of interesting conversation. Later that evening we sat holding hands on the front porch and Nora began to weep. She said she had prayed for me, then feared that I would never be coming back. Then she feared that I had been injured and would come back maimed.

She described her sleepless nights and hours and hours of being on her knees praying for my safe return. She laughed when she said she had donated a fortune to the votive candles box and probably worn out the kneeling pads praying. The following day I asked Nora when we would marry. She grew very serious and told me how much she had worried and even grieved when she thought I had been lost at sea. Somehow, she said, while she never gave up hope, she did come pretty close a few times. As the months lingered on, she said her fear grew stronger and stronger. Nora said she loved me very much but could not live the uncertain and lonely wife of a sea captain. I was crushed, but I understood her heartache. I thought it over for a few days, then I told Nora I would give up the sea. She was overjoyed and began to sing and weep at the same time. It was in 1871 that we agreed to marry before I sailed back to America. There, I promised I would buy a home, set up a business, then send for Nora.

We were married at St. Mary's Cathedral in Limerick with all the pomp and circumstance of a grand wedding of a well-to-do family. The bride wore white with purple flowers in her hair and a matching bouquet. I borrowed a tailcoat and pants from her dad. Nora's bridesmaids were all school chums. My best man was my old friend Mr. Larsen, who luckily was in Limerick on a ship for which he was now captain. The choir sang a selection of songs Nora had chosen. The organ was magnificent. When it hit a low note, you could almost feel the cathedral walls vibrating. The pew and the altar were decorated with flowers that matched Nora's bouquet. The priest wore a beautiful gold chasuble heavily decorated with religious symbols. The altar boys wore red cassocks and white surplices. Nora's dad gave her away and her mom and family sat in a front row. Most of the women were in tears. We were married at a mass with three priests attending. I think that may have been because Nora's family was well known in the Cathedral; she was respected for her beautiful singing at holiday masses. Everyone remembered her "Ave

Maria." The ring bearer was a beautiful little red-headed Irish girl dressed in pale blue and carrying our rings on a white pillow. The rings were secured with a strand of thread to ensure the little girl would not drop them on her way up the aisle. When the priest pronounced us man and wife, the organ roared the wedding march and the cathedral bells chimed wonderfully. We had just a weekend honeymoon, then I was off to return to America.

I had bought four matching dapple-grey Irish draft horses at the Limerick Horse Fair. Each one stood 18 hands and was a glorious specimen of horse flesh. I had gotten to know the breed when I was a boy. They were the strongest, yet the kindest, gentlest horses. And they were handsome and brave. There was an export agent at the fair who arranged to have them brought to my ship. In the meantime, Mr. Huntington had been loading a cargo of Irish linen, whiskey, cheese, and livestock. Our main cargo on this trip was wealthy people. While most of the Irish going to America sailed on what was known as a coffin ship, those that had money traveled in relative luxury on the clippers.

35

Traveling to America by ship during the Irish Famine could be quite perilous. In the mid-19th century, English landlords looking to evict penniless Irish tenants would pay to have them shipped to British North America. In many cases these ships were poorly built, crowded, disease-ridden, and short of food, supplies, and medical services. As a result, many Irish immigrants contracted diseases such as typhus, and many others died before reaching land. Of the 100,000 Irish that sailed to North America in 1847, one out of five died from disease or malnutrition. Appropriately, these treacherous sailing vessels became known as "coffin ships." I learned firsthand from a mate I knew who had actually sailed on a coffin ship. He described it as being jampacked with Irish immigrants and Scotch highlanders. The immigrants used the ships to escape the Great Irish Famine. While the ships crossed the Atlantic, many people died. The mate said the ships were really not much better than the slavers, except that the passengers were not in chains. Cruel, greedy captains denied the passengers access to water and food. Moreover, the ships were very crowded. The bad condition of the coffin ships caused Typhus epidemics. The owners of coffin ships did not break the laws, even though they provided only a small amount of water and food. The living space inside the coffin ships was limited too. The mortality rate for the people who used the coffin ships was 30 percent. However, the people considered it as the most economical way to cross the Atlantic Ocean. The bodies of those who died were thrown into the sea, while relatives often viewed sharks devouring the bodies of their loved ones.

One captain, James Attridge, discovered the major cause of disease on his coffin ships was contaminated straw bedding. He ordered that all straw bedding be changed daily. That reduced the spread of diseases and enabled him to be one of the very few captains on whose ship there was no loss of life. His ship made a voyage from County Kerry to Quebec on April 24, 1848, with 193 emigrants on board, as the effects of the Famine in Ireland raged. Between 1848 and 1855, the *Jeanie Johnston* made 16 voyages to North America, sailing to Quebec, Baltimore, and New York. On average, the length of the transatlantic journey was 47 days. The most passengers she ever carried was 254, from Tralee to Quebec on 17 April, 1852. Despite the number of passengers, and the long voyage, no crew or passenger lives were ever lost on board the *Jeanie Johnston*. This is generally attributed to the captain, James Attridge's not overloading the ship, and the presence of a qualified doctor, Richard Blennerhassett on board for the passengers.

I believe the key was having a qualified doctor on board. Larger naval vessels generally had a surgeon on board. Merchant ships usually did not. It became the job of the captain, in many cases, to be the surgeon. In my own experience I served that function many times when one of my crew became ill or was injured. I did not have any formal medical training, but I did have common sense and a wonderful book titled *The Ship Captains Medical Guide*. I think I saw a copy on just about every ship I sailed on after the British Merchant Shipping Act 1867 making it a law that owners and captains of vessels sailing under the British Flag had to carry medical stores to a standard defined in law. It required there to be onboard lime or lemon juice of a certain volume and standard, and to provide seamen with a certain standard of accommodations and working conditions. In addition, every ship was required to carry a medical book, containing instructions for dispensing the medical stores. In my experience prior to that law, it was up to the individual owners and captains to decide what if any medical stores and medical books were carried on any privately owned ship. No good captain worth his salt would sail without an adequate supply of both.

I made darn sure we had everything we might possibly need in a medical emergency and two copies of the Captain's Medical Guide. Anyone who has ever put to sea would have to know there were going to be medical emergencies, as sure as God made apples. My copy was well used, since I was the one called upon to act as the ship's surgeon. I vividly recall one time when on our way to Casablanca the mate called me to come look at a sick crewman. The poor fellow was writhing in agony and clutching the lower right side of his abdomen. He said the sharp pain hit him suddenly. It started around his naval and shifted to the right side of his abdomen. He said it was worse when he coughed and it hurt like hell when he tried to walk. His forehead was hot to the touch and his abdomen was swollen. I made some quick notes of his symptoms, instructed the mate to try to keep him comfortable and apply cool water-soaked cloths to his forehead. To make matters worse the ship was becalmed. The sails were slacked. I went back to my quarters to consult my Captain's Medical Guide. I learned quickly that the crewman was suffering from a ruptured appendix. Unless the ruptured appendix was removed immediately the man would probably die. I would have preferred to raise sail and rush to the nearest port, but the sails were slack, and we were drifting with the tide. There was no choice but for me to attempt to operate, a prospect I dreaded. The crewman was brought into my cabin and laid out on a table. We had some laudanum and rum to help him deal with the pain of the ruptured appendix and the pain from what I was about to attempt. My mate jury-rigged a lamp and sharpened the knives we had in our medical kit. The kit included a bottle of ether and a basket to put over the patient's nose and mouth.

While the mate got the crewman set up, I studied the procedure in the Medical Guide. When we were ready, I asked the mate to hold the book open to the pages I had studied so that he could read me a page if I asked for it. The one blessing of our being becalmed was that the ship was steady, making it better for me to start cutting away at the crewman. The first incision was more difficult than I had imagined. But in a short time, I got the hang of it. I had marked the spot where I needed to cut according to the directions in the guide. It referred to McBurney's point. Which is "a point on the lower right quadrant of the abdomen at which tenderness is maximal in cases of acute appendicitis. Acute appendicitis is characterized by the inflammation, infection, or swelling of the appendix. I made the transverse incision as directed, then asked the mate to read aloud the next steps. The guide predicted there would be squirting blood which I stopped by using some clamps that were included in our medical kit. One of the other mates helped by sponging out the blood to make it possible for me to find the infected appendix, which I did not have any idea what it looked like. I asked the mate to reread the description of what I was looking for. Step by step, I separated the rotting organ and tied off its connecting ducts. Then I sewed the wound back up as read to me by the mate. I applied bandages and said a prayer that my efforts at abdominal surgery would be successful. Fortunately, my stiches held and did not become infected. The wind picked up and by the time we reached the port of Casablanca in Morocco, my patient was feeling better. Once we reached port I had him taken to see a local doctor, who approved of my abdominal surgery.

On another voyage neophyte medical talents were once again called upon when one of the crew was cut open by the metal forelocks attached to the end of an errant yardarm he happened to get in the way of. Exactly how he accomplished that, I do not understand. He was bleeding across his back from his shoulder to his buttocks. There were ribs exposed and raw red flesh with blood bubbling out. I ordered my mate to pack the wound with a clean cloth and get the crewman to the galley table. The wound reminded me of one I saw back when I was boy on the farm and one of my dad's cows tore open its belly somehow. I watched the veterinarian clean and sew up the wound after he cauterized it with a hot blade. I did stitches the way I watched the vet do them, and, miraculously, the patient survived.

Not all of my surgical efforts worked out. One of the crewmen who did not report his leg injury came to me when his leg was turning greenish black. He did not survive, and I switched back to my role as captain and presided over his burial at sea. As we consigned his sailcloth-covered and weighted corpse into the sea I recited the age-old prayer,

> *"Lord God, by the power of your Word you stilled the chaos of the primeval seas, you made the raging waters of the Flood subside, and you calmed the storm on the Sea of Galilee.*
>
> *As we commit the earthly remains of our brother/sister [Full Name] to the deep, grant him/her peace and tranquility until that day when [name] and all who believe in you will be raised to the glory of new life promised in the waters of baptism. We ask this through Christ our Lord. Amen."*

Some of my fellow captains have accused me of being too friendly with my crew. Traditionally, a ship's captain has supreme power over every living soul on his ship. Legally that is absolutely true, but I am also a Christian, and I have my Catholic Bible to comfort me. It teaches me that I am a man no better and no worse than other men. I am in charge and I am obligated to punish crewmen if they deserve it, but I am also obligated to my lord Jesus Christ to be fair and honest. I will admit I respect many of the men under my command. My sailing master who is also my chief mate is a gifted man whose sailing skills are equal or better than my own. I see no reason why I should not share a pipe with a man like that, or have him as a friend. Certainly, I would share a dog watch with him gladly. I do not ever want to be remembered as is the infamous and cruel Captain Bligh.

36

O N A VOYAGE across the Atlantic, bringing cargo from Liverpool to New York, we sailed into what was probably one of the worst storms I had ever encountered at sea. It tested the ship and my crew beyond the endurance of many. It raged for nearly three days, then mercifully subsided. We were about halfway to New York, off course northerly by about 500 miles, licking our wounds and repairing the damage when the lookout shouted 'Ship ho." In a storm like we experienced there are no sails, there is no intentional movement, there is no navigation, you just try to survive. I was up near the helm when the call came. My cabin boy, a fine, smart young lad, brought me my glass and I searched in the direction the lookout had pointed.

Ahead off to starboard I spotted what appeared to be a ship without sails. As we approached, it became evident, she was without masts and not moving, but simply drifting in the rolling sea. I recognized her as one of the many lavish yachts around New York and European ports.

As we approached, I looked for signs of life. It seemed as if there were none, then a plume of smoke appeared at midship.

The sound of a whistle drifted across our bow. I told the mate to make ready to lower the longboat and form a crew to board the ship ahead. It became apparent that the smoke was a distress signal and not a ship on fire. When we reached a safe distance downwind of the ship, which by then, I was sure was a yacht, the mate and his crew rowed to the stricken yacht. In just a short time the first mate fired off a small rocket to signal to me that it was safe for our ship to approach. The seas had become quite calm, so it was safe to actually bring the yacht alongside. I sent a cabin boy down to the galley with instructions to start brewing a hearty broth and coffee. I was able to step across the gunnel of the stricken yacht. It was a tragic sight. All three of her masts had been snapped off. There were no remnants of any sails or yard. I assumed they had washed overboard. A bedraggled man, obviously the captain, made his way slowly across the deck to greet me. He reached out his hand, then he hugged me and said, "Thank God you found us, sir." In a kind of loud whisper, he said his name was Captain Roger Sean, master of the sailing yacht *Anna Christina* out of Newport. By then the broth had arrived and I offered some to the captain. He sipped it eagerly then took some coffee. He said they had not had food for nearly a week which was obvious from his weakened appearance and that of the crew members who gathered around us for the sustenance we offered. I inquired about the passengers, and he said he would take me to them. I assured the captain I was in no hurry and to take him time with his meal. Meanwhile my crew was passing out water, broth, and coffee to the crew. I asked my cabin boy to find out where the passengers were and asked the cook to provide the same to them. My mate and I looked over the ship to assess the damage and her seaworthiness. In addition to her having been dismasted, she had also lost her rudder and her anchor. On the whole, there seemed to be little risk of her sinking, but there was the possibility that a wave hitting her broadside could cause her to capsize. We decided there was no alternative but to take her in tow. Later that afternoon I met the passengers. The owner and his wife were in their lavishly decorated cabin aft. The captain introduced the owner as Mr. Thaddeus Thorndyke III and his wife Serena. He immediately thanked me and confided that he had despaired of being rescued because they were so far north of the shipping lanes, He thought he would never see America again. Mrs. Thorndyke expressed her deepest gratitude and told me we would be forever in her prayers. We left them to regain their strength and enjoy what was their first meal in a week. Casks of water and provisions were transferred to the yacht. We returned to our ship and made ready to hoist sails. A tow line was set up and in a short time, we were off and heading for New York. There was a good breeze and our sails billowed out, straining hard against the mast.

We sailed on for a week, then entered New York and took on a pilot. The pilot boat reported our situation and soon there were two steam tugs to take over the tow. We docked at South Street, then the tugs brought in the yacht and berthed her nearby. The plan was to move the damaged ship to a shipyard in Brooklyn as soon as the passengers had disembarked. When our ship was secure and offloading had begun, I walked over to the yacht. I was greeted at the gangway by Mr. Thorndyke who was looking considerably better than he did the last time I spoke with him. He gave me a hearty handshake and invited me to join him in his cabin. Over an hour's chat, he said he and his passengers would be moving to the New York Yacht Club for a few days, but would be dining that night. He invited my officers and me to join him for dinner at the club at 37 West 44th street in Manhattan. He arranged to have carriages pick us up. The dinner was lavish and included caviar, champagne, a glacé, oysters, squab, and all sorts of elegant foods, most of which we had rarely enjoyed. After dinner we adjourned to a billiard room where cigars and brandy were passed. While the officers engaged in a game of billiards, Mr. Thorndyke and I sat in nearby leather lounge chairs to enjoy some conversation. He again thanked me for the rescue and told me that if he could ever be of service to me, he would be there for me. He said, "I am forever in your debt." As we talked, he told me he was a close associate of M. Cornelius Vanderbilt in the railroad business. I asked if he knew my friend Thomas Edison and he said that he knew him quite well. He praised Edison as a genius. He was surprised to learn of Edison's humble beginnings and our being classmates as children.

It was an enjoyable evening for me and my officers, none of whom had ever enjoyed such an opulent dinner in such lavish surrounds. Before we parted, Mr. Thorndyke said that he would one day like to host a banquet to celebrate their rescue, at which I was to be the guest of honor.

The passenger accommodations on the *Lighting* were very comfortable indeed. We had room for twenty. During our voyage home the passengers dined with the officers every night. I got to know several of them. In fact, one of them told me about some property in Brooklyn that he owned. It seemed like an ideal property for the business I had in mind.

We ran into some storms crossing the Atlantic. The livestock did well but most of the passengers were seasick and missed several meals, with the exception of Mr. Bartholomew H. Bull. Bull was a seasoned sailor and actually was setting up a shipping company, a shipping line of his own with the new steam vessels. His plan was to bring fruit from South America and Florida to New York. We talked at length about his plans and mine. He suggested I start a company to ship his produce from the docks in Brooklyn to surrounding markets. By the time we reached New York, Mr. Bull and I had everything planned as to what my future would be. I supervised the offloading of the ship. I thanked the crew and advised the owner's agent that I was resigning. I recommended another captain I knew, and he got the job.

While I was in the city, I thought I might visit a bookstore I had come to know over the years. I looked through the books and came upon one by Mark Twain. The clerk said he was quite popular and had once worked on the Mississippi River boats. Since I had already actually worked on a riverboat, I thought it might be interesting to learn a little something more about river boats, so I bought Mark Twain's book The *Adventures of Huckleberry Finn*. I enjoyed it very much and found his comments about riverboats interesting. Twain's abhorrence of slavery and his willingness to protect his friend was very appealing. It conformed in many ways to my thinking. I thoroughly appreciated the story of the friendship and bond between Jim and Huck.

37

My PURSE FROM my work on the *Lighting* and what I had carefully saved over the years, provided me the funds to buy the property at 289 Pacific Street in the Red Hook section of Brooklyn. There was a grand three-story brick Victorian and a large barn in the rear with enough room for the four Dapple Greys and room for expansion if I bought more. I found a sturdy wag and had it painted orange. Then I had it lettered with large silver letters reading PATRIC SWEENEY HAULING. The next thing I did was book passage for Nora on the next ship leaving Limerick. I wrote to mom and dad and invited them to come live with us in the house in Brooklyn. It has plenty of room and they could have a whole floor to themselves. The invitation included my brother and sister as well.

While I waited for Nora to arrive from Ireland, I found myself reading more. I bought another of Mark Twain's books one titled *The Adventures of Tom Sawyer*. I identified with the character in the book because I was a farm boy at one time back in Ohio. He wrote about the joys of childhood when the world is full of wonders and children are free of the heavy responsibilities of adulthood. I felt Mark Twain was writing about his own boyhood, growing up in the small town of Hannibal, Missouri, right on the edge of the great Mississippi River. I felt he was writing about me. Tom is a town boy. If he lived on a subsistence farm like the majority of Americans in those times, he would not have the freedom he enjoys in this novel. Farm boys were put to work at an early age, and much of their work consisted of plowing behind a horse or mule. They were often called "plowboys." I was as fortunate as Tom because I lived on my parents' farm.

I kept busy getting the house ready for Nora's arrival. Luckily, I got some help from Mrs. Archibald Bull. She knew where to buy curtains, who to get to paint the walls, she knew plumbers and had all manner of connections. All written down in her little black book. She was a tremendous help in my getting to the house ready for the arrival of my beautiful Nora. One day while she was choosing some upholstery fabric for a living room couch, she noticed my book by Mark Twain. She was delighted to learn that I was reading it. She said she had discovered his work a few months earlier and really enjoyed his books. She recommended I read some of his articles in the Atlantic Month.

38

M Y PURSE FROM my work on the *Lighting* and what I had carefully saved over the years, provided me the funds to buy the property at 289 Pacific Street in the Red Hook section of Brooklyn. There was a grand three-story brick Victorian and a large barn in the rear with enough room for the four Dapple Greys and room for expansion if I bought more. I found a sturdy wag and had it painted orange. Then I had it lettered with large silver letters reading PATRIC SWEENEY HAULING. The next thing I did was book passage for Nora on the next ship leaving Limerick. I wrote to mom and dad and invited them to come live with us in the house in Brooklyn. It has plenty of room and they could have a whole floor to themselves. The invitation included my brother and sister as well.

While I waited for Nora to arrive from Ireland, I found myself reading more. I bought another of Mark Twain's books one titled *The Adventures of Tom Sawyer*. I identified with the character in the book because I was a farm boy at one time back in Ohio. He wrote about the joys of childhood when the world is full of wonders and children are free of the heavy responsibilities of adulthood. I felt Mark Twain was writing about his own boyhood, growing up in the small town of Hannibal, Missouri, right on the edge of the great Mississippi River. I felt he was writing about me. Tom is a town boy. If he lived on a subsistence farm like the majority of Americans in those times, he would not have the freedom he enjoys in this novel. Farm boys were put to work at an early age, and much of their work consisted of plowing behind a horse or mule. They were often called "plowboys." I was as fortunate as Tom because I lived on my parents' farm.

I kept busy getting the house ready for Nora's arrival. Luckily, I got some help from Mrs. Archibald Bull. She knew where to buy curtains, who to get to paint the walls, she knew plumbers and had all manner of connections. All written down in her little black book. She was a tremendous help in my getting to the house ready for the arrival of my beautiful Nora. One day while she was choosing some upholstery fabric for a living room couch, she noticed my book by Mark Twain. She was delighted to learn that I was reading it. She said she had discovered his work a few months earlier and really enjoyed his books. She recommended I read some of his articles in the Atlantic Month.

39

MY PURSE FROM my work on the *Lighting* and what I had carefully saved over the years, provided me the funds to buy the property at 289 Pacific Street in the Red Hook section of Brooklyn. It was a grand three-story brick Victorian with a large barn in the rear with enough room for the four Dapple Greys and room for expansion if I bought more. I found a sturdy wagon and had it painted orange, then lettered with large silver letters reading PATRICK SWEENEY HAULING. I booked passage for Nora on the next ship leaving Limerick. I wrote to Mom and Dad and invited them to come live with us in the house in Brooklyn. It has plenty of room and they could have a whole floor to themselves. The invitation included my brother and sister as well.

While I waited for Nora to arrive from Ireland, I found myself reading more. I bought another of Mark Twain's books, one titled *The Adventures of Tom Sawyer*. I identified with the character in the book because I was a farm boy at one time back in Ohio. He wrote about the joys of childhood when the world is full of wonders and children are free of the heavy responsibilities of adulthood. I felt Mark Twain was writing about his own boyhood, growing up in the small town of Hannibal, Missouri, right on the edge of the great Mississippi River. I felt he was writing about me. Tom is a town boy. If he lived on a subsistence farm like the majority of Americans in these times, he would not have the freedom he enjoys in this novel. Farm boys were put to work at an early age, and much of their work consisted of plowing behind a horse or mule. They were often called "plowboys." I was as fortunate as Tom because I lived on my parents' farm.

I kept busy getting the house ready for Nora's arrival. Luckily, I got some help from Mrs. Archibald Bull. She knew where to buy curtains, whom to get to paint the walls. She knew plumbers and had all manner of connections--all written down in her little black book. She was a tremendous help in my getting to the house ready for the arrival of my beautiful Nora. One day while she was choosing some upholstery fabric for a living room couch, she noticed my book by Mark Twain. She was delighted to learn that I was reading it. She said she had discovered his work a few months earlier and really enjoyed it. She recommended I read his articles in the *Atlantic Monthly*.

40

IT TOOK TWO months for Nora to join me. Her voyage was good, and she brought along a large trousseau and lots of furniture. Nora quickly adapted to life in America. I took her to her first opera, and she was thrilled. She enjoyed visiting restaurants and theaters in Manhattan. One Sunday we went to mass at the new cathedral being built on Fifth Ave in Manhattan. They called it Saint Patrick's, but I assured Nora it was not named after me. There were still stone masons working on the steeples, but mass was being held anyway. She was thrilled and likened it to St Mary's in Limerick.

Then one day I received a hand delivered letter from Mr. Thorndyke. It was an invitation to attend a banquet at his home in Newport, Rhode Island. He had also arranged for train transportation and prepared rooms for us at his home. Nora was delighted and eagerly accepted the invitation. Nora insisted I go to Brooks brothers and buy a tuxedo. She planned to wear the gowns and mantilla I bought for her in Spain. It was my first visit to H. & D. H. Brooks & Co. on the northeast corner of Catherine and Cherry Streets in Manhattan. It was in fact the first time I had ever bought a tuxedo.

The affair at the Thorndyke home was truly lavish, as were our accommodations. At the banquet, Mr. Thorndyke introduced me as the guest of honor and told the gathering the story of the rescue. He then presented me with a lifetime pass for my entire family on the New York Central Railroad and its connecting railroads. It was an awesome gift because it enabled me and my whole family to travel everywhere. Somehow Mrs. Thorndyke discovered that Nora sang and invited her to sing her Ave Maria at the banquet. The applause was deafening, and I was bursting with pride not only in her singing but also in her beauty. The audience chanted "more, more" and Nora obliged with some of popular songs of the day. Then we danced the night away. We spent all three days at Newport, then traveled back to Brooklyn. I believe that for Nora and me it was the most incredible, decadent weekend we had ever enjoyed. It was a glimpse into the lifestyles of what are known as the robber barons.

AFTER MY PARENTS passed, my brother John and my sister Bertha came to live with us. My sweet Nora and my sister hit it off from the start. My brother came to work for me in the business and I was glad to have him. I could not have been happier. I had my family, whom I really had not seen much of from the time I left home at age 14. And my beautiful Nora. As a wedding gift, I bought Nora a grand piano that we put in the living room of the house on Pacific Street. I cherished those Sunday evenings with Nora playing and singing in the living room. Every Sunday we gathered for a family dinner and Nora entertained us after dinner.

Nora Mary Adamson Sweeny is my precious wife. She was born on March 17th, 1844, in County Limerick, Ireland. Her father's name was Samuel and mother's name was Anna Mauna. Her voice has just a hint of Irish laughter and the ring of joy. I am still mystified and humbled by her acceptance of my proposal of marriage. I know from conversations I have had over the years with members of her family that she had no end of invitations to marry from numerous eligible young Irish bachelors who courted her back in Limerick, especially when word got out that I was possibly lost at sea. Describing Nora as beautiful is inadequate. She is a real-life version of Sandro Botticelli's Birth of Venus. From her long auburn hair to the tips of her toes, she is exquisite. Nora can sit horse, clear a 4-foot jump riding sidesaddle, drive a team, shoot a pistol, load any gun, shoot a rifle, hit a bird on the wing, bring down a buck and transform it into a sumptuous dinner. She sews, knits and crochets. The hats she creates set the church pews in motion. She is my love, my life, and the absolute best part of me. She is and has always been my inspiration and my conscience. Nora is the reason for my very being. She sings like an angel and plays the piano and organ beautifully, a skill she has passed on to our daughter Annie. Nora heals our wounds and soothes our hurt feelings. She is the one who has enabled me to control my fiery temper. She always presents a reasonable argument to cool my timbers. Nora reads the daily newspaper from cover to cover. She fills me in on the news of the day over dinner. I dreaded the times when a story would appear in the paper about women's suffrage. Nora is an advocate of a woman's right to vote and would sometimes get all worked up about it, which meant dinner got cold. Whether she is happy or angry, she is beautiful.

Because of the growing population and because of my association with Mr. Bull, business in Brooklyn was very good, right from the start. In a short time, I bought another used wagon and four more dapple grey horses. I was thinking life could not be more perfect. Adding to our joy, little Annie Josephine

Sweeney was born on December 22, 1879. She was the image of her mother and just the sweetest baby. Sunday evenings lying in her crib while Nora sang and played the piano, she seemed to know exactly what was going on and grinned throughout. She never cried when Nora was singing. Annie's brother John Edward arrived a year later.

Before long, my sister Bertha married a fine young attorney and moved into a lovely house on Montague Street in Brooklyn. They often joined us for Sunday dinner. My brother John remained a bachelor for several years, enjoying the New York night life and the beautiful women who were very much a part of it. John loved sports and regularly went to Madison Square Garden. The Garden, as he called it, was owned by William Vanderbilt, and was constantly abuzz with sporting events, as well as P. T. Barnum's circus, which was brought to Madison Square Garden each year. Located at the northeast corner of 26th Street and Madison Avenue, it hosted a variety of diverse activities: dog shows, cattle displays, political conventions, circuses, theater, opera, balls, religious revivals, and boxing matches. John loved them all and the ladies he took with him. Nora and I attended the circus as soon as little Annie was old enough to enjoy it. I think Annie and I enjoyed the menagerie just about as well as the circus. Young John loved it too. He was enthralled with the live animals and the clowns. Annie did not like the clowns at all.

42

WHILE MY BROTHER John was helping me run the business, I thought it was about time I took my little family on a vacation. We had our train passes, thanks to Mr. Thorndyke, so Nora started thinking about some possible trips. The following summer we journeyed to Gettysburg, Pennsylvania. An avid student of history, Nora read that in 1864 the Gettysburg Battlefield Memorial Association and other veterans' associations acquired land for Civil War memorials and preservation. I had always wanted to visit that historic place, so we did exactly that. Prior to the trip, we read up on what happened there. Gettysburg National Cemetery is the final resting place for more than 3,500 Union soldiers killed in the Battle of Gettysburg. It was a major turning point in the Civil War. At the cemetery's dedication on November 19, 1863, President Abraham Lincoln rose to deliver "a few appropriate remarks," now known as the Gettysburg Address. His two-minute speech served as a reminder of the sacrifices of war and the necessity of holding the Union together. Interestingly enough, there was another famous speaker at the podium who spoke for two hours, yet no one remembers who he was or what he said. We made sure the children learned that former Secretary of State Edward Everett was the man and that he gave an important speech urging the North and the South to come together as one great nation. One day after the consecration, he wrote to the president and asked for a copy of the little address. "I should be glad," Everett wrote, "if I could flatter myself that I came as near to the central idea of the occasion in two hours as you did in two minutes."

We engaged a tour guide and carriage and visited Little Round Top, The Devil's Den and all the historic sights. The guide showed us the spot where General Robert E Lee sat on his horse Traveler while commanding his troops with General James Longstreet at his side. Then he took us to the site where college professor turned soldier Colonel Joshua Chamberlin held the high ground while the Southern troops relentlessly attacked. In the end his union troops captured the attacking troops with the rifle for which they had run out of ammunition. The guide related the heroic stories of Generals Buford, Picket, Hood, and many more. He said there was a total of fifty-three Confederate and sixty-seven Union generals who fought there. Gettysburg was a somber place that made a deep impression on us all. It brought home to us in a kind of vivid reality the awful tragedy of war and the inhumanity of battle where the cream of American manhood slaughtered each other in bloody conflict. It is, as Abraham Lincoln said so eloquently there in the hot sun at the Gettysburg battlefield —*"We cannot consecrate—we cannot hallow—this ground. The brave men, living and dead, who struggled here, have consecrated it, far above our poor power to add or detract."*

43

Nora and I were avid theatergoers. We enjoyed plays, musical entertainment, and vaudeville. There was a wonderful theater not far from our home. The Brooklyn Theatre opened on October 2, 1871, and stood near the southeast corner of Washington and Johnson streets, one block north of Brooklyn's City Hall. I remember in 1876 we attended a play titled *The Two Orphans*. It was a historical play by the French writers Adolphe d'Ennery and Eugène Cormon. Nora loved it, as did the Brooklyn Daily Eagle. Their review in the evening issue read,

> On a scale as to human and mechanical interpretation, which certainly made a near approach to the common idea of perfection. The audience, although in point of numbers, it was scarcely on a par with the claims of the occasion, was visibly moved during the progress of the play and must have left the theatre with an impression of the performance such as in itself ought to prove no bad advertisement of its excellence. The applause was frequent, hearty and spontaneous, and in response to it the curtain had to be raised after nearly every one of the seven tableaux, by which the action of the piece is articulated…The whole representation, therefore, was one which exacts the acknowledgement that little can be said of it except in the way of praise.

Frankly, I was happy that Nora enjoyed it so much. The play had originally been presented in French in Paris. It was set during the French Revolution, and dealt with the hardship of those times. It was not really my cup of tea. I think I would rather have attended one of the shows presented by Mark Twain.

ONE YEAR WE took a vacation on a boat sailing up the beautiful Hudson River. The boat, belonging to a friend of mine, had very nice accommodations and the whole family was very comfortable. We marveled at the beauty of the Hudson River. The boat stopped at West Point, where we had a chance to tour the military academy. We watched a stunningly beautiful review of the cadets with the US Army band. I have to admit that I love a parade and all the pomp and circumstance that is West Point. The beat of the drums, the crash of the symbols, and the blare of trumpets stir my heart. The sound of a bugler playing the haunting sounds of taps can bring me close to tears.

We stayed overnight at a nearby West Point Hotel. Built in 1829, it was located near the Plain on Trophy Point. A plaque in the lobby detailed the history of the hotel. The West Point Hotel served the Academy for years and hosted a long list of dignitaries such as Robert E. Lee, Ulysses S. Grant, Stonewall Jackson, Winfield Scott, William Tecumseh Sherman, Washington Irving, Edgar Allen Poe, and Hames Whistler. If only the walls could talk, what delightful stories they would tell.

The next day we proceeded on the boat north to Albany where I felt at home among the many ships. Annie and John enjoyed reading the home port display. I explained to them that I had been a "hoggie" as a young boy working my way to New York. I had read that back in 1817, the New York Mayor De Witt Clinton persuaded the state legislature to authorize loans for $7 million to build a canal from Buffalo on the eastern shore of Lake Erie, to the upper Hudson, passing through the Mohawk Valley region.

To traverse the canal, back in my day, we used a team of horses or mules to transfer to a canal boat that was pulled through the canal by a team of mules. I was extremely interested in seeing how they cross nowadays and how the new locks were made. I still marvel at how the boats are lowered from one level to the next. I wanted Nora and the kids to understand how the valves that control the flow of water into and out of the locks worked. The family enjoyed the trip immensely. Soon we were back in Brooklyn and back to work.

45

ANNIE STARTED ATTENDING school that fall. She was reluctant at first, but very quickly began interacting with the other children. John was already attending and loved it. Our church was the Cathedral Basilica of St. James, where we attended mass faithfully every Sunday and on holy days. The next year we vacationed on a sailing vessel that belonged to a friend of mine. George Bruns was in the same business as I was, but he also had ships that delivered fruit and produce to Washington, D.C. It was a very nice trip along the coast of New Jersey, then up into the Potomac River. The kids loved sailing and I have to say I felt right at home once again. The captain let Annie and John steer the ship for a while with the help of the first mate and they were thrilled. Nora enjoyed standing in the bow with the wind in her hair and being sprayed on occasion as the bow dug into a wave. Often, I would just sit on the capstan and admire her beauty. We sailed down to Cape Charles, then north up the Chesapeake to the Potomac River.

We spent a night on Tangier Island in Chesapeake Bay. I learned that the War of 1812, which pitted the United States, Great Britain, and their allies against each other over three years, turned into an opportunity for enslaved African Americans to advocate for their freedom. Between the summers of 1813 and 1814, 4,000-5,000 fled to the side of the British, in the hopes of securing freedom and safe passage for themselves and their families. The British established Fort Albion on Tangier Island off the coast of Virginia in the Chesapeake Bay in April 1814, and nearly 1,000 slaves found refuge at the site. There were also lots of skip jacks' boats berthed on the small island. Oysters and crabs were being shipped daily from Tangier Island.

We spent the night and visited a very primitive restaurant they called the Crab Shack. I ordered oysters on the half-shell and introduced them to my wife. The kids would have no part of them. They preferred fried breaded soft-shell crabs and especially fried potatoes and corn. John bravely tried a raw oyster but gagged when he tried to swallow it. The captain demonstrated how to pick apart a steamed blue crab that when cooked was very red. It was a lot of work, but he used a wooden mallet to crack the shells and a small fork to pick out the crab meat that turned out to be delicious, especially when dipped in melted butter. Nora had a little trouble picking out the meat, so I wound up picking the crabs and piling the meat on her plate. Anne picked at the steamed crabs. John took on the task with a vengeance. He loved banging a claw with the mallet and then picking out the meat.

46

Τ HE SHIP LEFT Tangier at daybreak, and we were heading for the entrance to the Potomac. I was right up there with the captain enjoying the sunrise, very red and beautiful when viewed on the Chesapeake. It seemed as if the entire sky was painted orange-red. Later that afternoon we docked just down the road from the mall. The owner of the boat has a home just up the hill from the dock and we stayed there.

In Washington, D.C. a horse-drawn carriage took us to the hotel where we enjoyed a fine meal. Bright and early the next morning we embarked on a carriage tour of the capital. The first stop was the majestic Washington Monument standing some 135 feet in the air. The next stop was the Smithsonian Institution, an incredible museum documenting the history of America. The kids loved it and we stayed for hours. The highlight was the Capitol. It was beautifully planned by the French engineer Pierre Charles L'Enfant. He located the Capitol at the elevated east end of the mall, on the brow of what was then called Jenkins' Hill. The site was, in L'Enfant's words, "a pedestal waiting for a monument It is an incredibly beautiful building.

The history of the United States Capitol Building begins in 1793. Since then, the U.S. Capitol has been built, burnt, rebuilt, extended, and restored. It was a work in progress when we visited. Next on the tour was Mount Vernon. I found a printed brochure about Mount Vernon and was so impressed I saved it for years. I quote it here.

> *Mount Vernon was more than George Washington's home; it was his project. From the time the Virginia property came into his hands in 1754, when he was a bold and desperately ambitious young major in the Virginia militia, until his death two weeks shy of a new century in 1799, by which time he was the embodiment of American grandeur and rectitude, he never stopped tinkering with the place. For much of his life, Washington was away from home on urgent business, and so he directed most of the work on Mount Vernon by letter. But his correspondence is so filled with appraising references to wallpaper, nails, paint, hinges, locks, putty, and glass that the man who emerges from it seems as much a frustrated handyman as the presiding figure of his age.*

Even when things were at their bleakest, when his new country was falling apart before his eyes, Washington never lost interest in his fixer-upper on the Potomac River. In September, 1776, in one of the first crucial engagements of the Revolutionary War, the colonial army suffered a humiliating rout on Manhattan Island, fleeing in panic from the invading British and Hessian forces as Washington rode among his troops on horseback trying futilely to beat them back into action with his riding whip.

"If I were to wish the bitterest curse to an enemy on this side of the grave," he wrote to Lund Washington, the cousin who managed Mount Vernon in his absence, "I should put him in my stead with my feelings." But in the same letter, penned in a dark hour when his cause seemed hopeless and he felt his reputation sagging into disgrace, Washington was still issuing instructions for work on his dream house. "The chimney in the new room should be exactly in the middle of it," he instructed Lund, with a whiplash change of tone and topic, "Doors and everything else to be exactly answerable and uniform—in short, I would have the whole executed in a masterly manner."

The mansion that Washington continually remodeled on his 8,000-acre estate sits on a high bluff above the Potomac River. Washington's "Home House" imparts a sense of remoteness and serenity. Washington seems to somehow be there like the fireflies on the sloping lawn or the swaying branches of the ages-old pecan tree that towers above the southern wing of the mansion.

The commodious high-ceilinged ground-level porch that faces the river and runs from one end of the house to the other provides an awesome view. It is a beguilingly informal and versatile space that George and Martha Washington often used as an open-air dining room. An extensive veranda of the kind that has become a mainstay of North American domestic architecture. It is an ingenious way of taking advantage of Mount Vernon's splendid location, but at the time the piazza was built, nothing of the sort had yet been seen in England or the New World. The supremely practical George Washington thought it up on his own.

IN DECEMBER OF 1876, Nora and I had a chance to see the arm and torch of what one day was going to be a massive statue on Bedloe's Island in New York Harbor. We bought a miniature statue when we exited through a little gift shop bursting with souvenirs. The statue was conceived and designed by Frederick August Bertoldi and was to be a gift to the American people from the people of France. It took ten years to get the money and build the statue in France. It had to be disassembled and shipped to America, then reassembled. In early October of 1886, we received an invitation from Mr. Thaddeus Thorndyke III to join him on his yacht for the dedication on October 28, 1886, of what was to become known as the Statue of Liberty. Mr. Thorndyke's yacht picked us up at a pier just off Columbia Street, only a few blocks from our home. Rounding the battery, we could see the statue. It was a majestic sight. Some 300 feet tall, it was shiny copper with a golden flame atop the torch. Nora and I climbed to the top of the torch and looked down on New York Harbor as we had never seen it before.

During my days at sea, I had several visits to the Port of Paris in France. Fortunately, I usually had a shipmate who was as interested as I was in seeing the sights of this magnificent city. The Eiffel Tower had not yet been constructed, although stories were circulating that it was in the planning stages. Paris was amazing. Just walking along the Champs-Élysées was a thrill. Of course, the food in Paris is like no other. My mom's Irish cooking was far simpler than the gourmet food in Paris. I remember reading somewhere that while Thomas Jefferson was living in Paris he developed a great appreciation for the cuisine. So much so, that he sent one of his servants, John Hemmings, to the leading culinary school to learn how to cook in the French style. When they returned to Monticello, Jefferson enjoyed French cooking and could entertain his many guests with authentic French cuisine. Hemmings was the first American chef to be trained in Paris. We visited the Louvre Museum, walked along the bank of the Seine River, and gaped at the wonders of the Versailles Palace. And, we, too had the opportunity to visit several of the bistros. There were times when we would sit on a bench and enjoy the passing parade of beautiful women. The crowning glory was Notre Dame Cathedral. Its sheer size is breathtaking, its history remarkable, and its beauty stunning.

48

THINGS WERE GETTING really busy in and around the East River and our neighborhood on Pacific Street. John Roebling had been commissioned to build a bridge across the East River from lower Manhattan to Brooklyn. Early in 1870 two massive wooden caissons were constructed at the Webb & Bell shipyard in Greenpoint, Brooklyn, and were launched into the river on March 19, 1870. The first was placed at the Brooklyn side and was to form the base for one of the two massive stone suspension towers. The commissions were placed upside down and lowered into the mud.

The offices of John and Washington Roebling were located at 89 Hicks Street at Carberry Street, not far from our home. Roebling could view the construction of the bridge from his office window. Compressed air was pumped into the caisson where workers entered the space to dig out the sand until the caisson sank into the bedrock. The actual granite base stones were placed on the caisson to form the footing for the towers.

Workers soon began suffering from what has come to be known as caisson disease or the bends. I remember reading a story in the newspaper about how John Roebling was injured when he somehow got his foot banged up on the job site. It said he was being treated with hydrotherapy. I can't count the number of injuries I treated at sea. On smaller ships, we never had a surgeon. If a man was cut, "cookie" would crank up the stove and heat a blade until it glowed red. Cookie, the crew sometimes called him "Doc", or I, would quickly press the red-hot blade to the open wound to seal it. The aroma of burning human flesh smelled awful but it generally worked. They call it cauterizing. The patient would give out an ungodly scream.

I can imagine the pain Roebling must have endured when his foot was crushed. Then a while later I heard that his son Washington had taken over the job of supervising until he came down with caisson's disease. The men who were working in the caisson were suffering from the bends. It was called the bends because it caused the joints to bend. John Roebling stayed too long, and he was afflicted. It must have hit him pretty hard because he had to supervise the rest of the work from his window using a telescope. His wife Emily had studied engineering, so she could help, and she finished the bridge after he died. Later on, we heard that there was a big scandal about the bridge. Ironically, they gave the job to Roebling because his company made the best cable in the world. Then the boys in Tammy decided it would be wise to have someone else make the cable so Roebling would not be tempted to use inferior cable or use too much. It turned out that the crooks who supplied the cable did just that by setting up an inspection station and passing the same cable through it over and over again while sending the inferior cable directly to the site. I remember seeing wagon loads of cable moving down the street headed for the bridge site. Luckily Roebling anticipated they would do that and specified the cable to be ten times stronger than needed. Neither of the Roeblings lived to see their bridge finished.

The opening of the Brooklyn Bridge was a grand affair with all kinds of politicians and celebrities there for the first walk across what was one of the first bridges to use steel cable. People were leery of this new type of bridge and had heard stories about bridges collapsing. P.T. Barnum got into the act and suggested he parade some of his elephants across ahead of the people to demonstrate its safety. On May 17, 1884, Barnum marched 21 elephants across the bridge, along with 17 camels.

Not long after the opening, a newspaper article reported that on May 30, 1884, a woman tripped and fell on the steps up to the bridge, prompting another woman to scream and crowds to push forward. Then, panic: Those following were in turn pushed over and, in a moment, the narrow stairway was choked with human beings, piled one on top of the other, who were being crushed to death. In a few minutes, 12 persons were killed, 7 injured so seriously that their lives are despaired of, and 28 others more or less severely wounded." We started using the bridge with our wagons and for pleasure trips into Manhattan. It saved us a great deal of time getting to South Street.

49

ONE CHRISTMAS I bought Nora a one-horse sleigh known as an equestrian cutter. She already had her horse and had been riding since she was a little girl back in Ireland. When it snowed starting in October it became dangerous to use our surrey. In 1888 there was a blizzard that tied up the city for days. It was so deep we could not get the horses out of the barn. Of course, once we got the snow cleared and the streets were passable, we had a lot of fun on the cutter. There was not any business going on, so it was a sort of fun vacation. The barn behind our house on Pacific Street is also the barn where I kept the big draft horses for my trucking business. As the business grew, I added stalls to accommodate more draft horses and hay and feed storage. At the same time, I built a smaller barn for the horse we used for Nora's sleigh and the surrey. It included a storage area for the vehicles and a nice-sized tack for our saddles and tack. When Annie was 8 years old, I bought her a Connemara Pony. As a young girl just learning to talk, she used to say Mahoney instead of Pony, so we all agreed to name her pony Mahoney.

50

As a surprise anniversary present to my darling wife Nora, I arranged for us to visit Nora's home in Ireland. My brother John had the business well in hand and was perfectly capable of running it while I was away. Through my friend Mr. Bull, I arranged first-class accommodations on the luxury steamer *RMS Umbria*. At one of the dinners I attended with Mr. Bull, he had praised the service he had experienced traveling on Cunard ships. I agreed. Cunard went all out to make passengers comfortable—even childen, with special menus for them and planned entertainment. The voyage was a perfect delight. Captain Theodore Cook was the master and the senior captain for Cunard Lines. We ate dinner at the captain's table several times. He extended me every courtesy as a fellow captain. He gave me access to the pilot house at any time and encouraged me to visit. Captain Cook and I had some fascinating conversations over a pipe and brandy. The bridge of a steamship like *Etruria* is a uniquely wonderful place to get to know someone. *Etruria* was one of the last two Cunard ocean liners fitted with auxiliary sails. *Umbria* was the last express steamship to be built with a compound engine for a North Atlantic route. There I was at home on a sailing vessel that also had a steam engine. *Umbria* and her running mate *Etruria* were record-breakers. The largest liners then in service, they ran between Liverpool and New York. There were two large funnels amidship and three large steel masts. She was barkentine-rigged. It was truly a luxury ship, even equipped with innovative refrigeration. The Umbria was a kind of floating showcase of Victorian style. The public rooms were full of ornately carved furniture; heavy velvet curtains hung in all the rooms, and they were decorated with the bric-a-brac that period fashion dictated. These rooms and the first-class cabins were situated on the promenade, upper, saloon, and main deck. Nora enjoyed the music room and took full advantage of the opportunity to show off her talents, which once heard, her voice echoing through the hall, gathered a crowd. There was also a smoking room for gentlemen and separate dining rooms for first and second-class passengers. Cunard registered *Umbria* at the port of Liverpool.

I think the children enjoyed the trip most of all. Captain Cook invited us all to visit the bridge and later that day he had the chief engineer give me a tour of the engine room with its massive boilers and maze of gauges and valves. The engineer seemed most proud of the ship telegraph, a shiny brass stanchion with two levers on top that was used to communicate orders from the bridge to the engine room. Nearby was a speaking tube which enabled to cabin to talk to the engineer. It was a very far cry from even my newest sailing vessel. Lastly, I was introduced to the sailing master which on the ship with an engine might seem superfluous. However, he explained that at times the ship was very much dependent on its sails.

We had good weather all the way. The Adamson family was waiting on the pier as the ship, guided by tugs entered its berth in Limerick. They greeted us at the foot of the gangway, with hugs, tears, and kisses. We had not seen any of the family since our wedding. Nora's dad had passed away but pretty much the rest of the family with a few young additions were present. Nora delighted in introducing John and Annie to the family. They had a surrey to bring us all back to their home. It was still as lovely as ever. The dinner was a grand affair with all of the family enjoying roast pig, potatoes, cabbage, and a fine dessert of cheese assorted fruit, and coffee. Nora made plans to take the children on a tour of the area including Castle Carrigogunnell,

I chose to stay home, relax, and get to know Nora's family. When Nora and the children returned from their sightseeing trip, she announced that since it was fall and fox hunting season she would like to ride to hounds. She invited me to join in the hunt but when I protested that I did not have the proper attire she said she had that all figured out. She had obtained the loan of proper attire for me through her brother. Any thoughts I might have had of not hunting soon vanished. and I accepted the invitation. to join the hunt. Since I was not a member, I was required to wear a black Melton jacket while Nora, who had been a whipper-in before we married, was still a life member of the hunt and was privileged to wear scarlet with the hunt's colors. Fortunately, we had been regular riders in Prospect Park, so I was no stranger to the saddle. Nora road astride rather than sidesaddle because she was a whipper-in. She sat her horse exceedingly well. We met at the next farm over for a stirrup cup, then hounds were cast at ten o'clock. The Master of Foxhounds had a fine 20 couple of Irish fox hounds out for the day's sport. His huntsman was a professional in that his full-time job was the care and training of the hounds as well as hunting them, I hadn't taken a fence since my days back on our farm in Port Huron and was a little leery about the prospect. Nora assured me that I would have no problem. She added that I looked perfectly wonderful in my hunting attire. The Huntsman blew his horn and gathered the hounds around him and headed off in search of a scent. We all followed the Field Master who was riding behind the Master of Foxhounds. It was a beautiful sight to see them all resplendent in scarlet. The whippers-in, including Nora, wore stirrup leather across their chests. It is a symbol of their position in the hunt as well as a handy remedy for any of the riders who may have broken a stirrup leather. At first, we walked through a field then another one. At that point, the Huntsman blew several quick notes on his horn, and we broke into a trot. A shiver of fear went through my body as we approached a rail fence. I gathered up a handful of the horse's mane, dug my feet into the stirrups, and hoped the horse would manage the jump better than I could. To my amazement, I sailed over the fence all in one piece. We were on a line and the Huntsman blew his horn repeatedly. It was probably the most exciting ride on a horse I have ever experienced. The fences became easier and before long I was enjoying every one of them. The hounds lost the scent, and the hunt came to a standstill. The Huntsman tried several different casts with no luck, when suddenly Nora galloped up from the headland and pointed her whip to the place where she had seen the fox. The Huntsman directed the hounds into the cover and in moments was blowing his horn in the rapid beat that signified his hounds were back on a line. Moments later he shouted, "Tally Ho" and we were off again at the gallop. The chase went on over several farms and through some stable yards. Finally, the fox went to the ground, and the hunt was over. It was a thrilling afternoon that I enjoyed immensely. We went to a nearby inn where we had agreed to meet for a hunt breakfast, even though it was more like 3 pm. The breakfast of bangers and mash, pork pies, broiled kidneys pulled fowl, tongues, quenelles, and croquettes of rice and ham, was delectable, perhaps because we were all very hungry. We did not catch a fox that day but that did not matter all. Renard, the old red fox had once again outsmarted the hounds as he had for many years and he would live to again provide another day of sport. It was the thrill of the chase that makes foxhunting as the poet said, "The sport of kings, the image of war without guilt."

I for one was worn out after a day's sport. Nora, on the other hand, was ready to attend a dance at St. Mary's. Of course, Nora prevailed, and I attempted to dance despite my aching muscles. The children danced and there was a display of traditional Celtic step dancing which the children found delightful. Nora promised them she would instruct them in the dance when we returned to America, Our visit lasted four weeks during which time we attended the Limerick Horse Sales where Annie fell in love with a Shetland pony. The Horse Sales were a unique treat for me. There were dozens of horses from fancy cart ponies to massive draft horses. I watched with great interest as the auction was conducted quite differently from the way it is done in America. In Limerick there is no auctioneer, the bargaining is done on a one-to-one basis with a smack of the hand signaling a deal. There were wagons and carts, harnesses, and many other horse-related items. I bought a traditional Irish jaunting car and then endeavored to get it shipped home. John decided he wanted to be a whipper-in after he watched the hunt as a hilltopper. In the course of those four weeks, I gained a love of Ireland I had only heard about from a pier in Limerick.

Before long it was time to say farewell and to voyage back to America. Fortunately, we had booked passage on the *Umbria*. Captain Cook greeted us as we boarded and once again was a gracious host and wonderful company on our trip home.

On those quiet evenings at sea, after Nora and the children had retired for the evening, Captain Cook and I had some time together enjoying a smoke and a glass or two in the smoking room. He was a very interesting, if reserved, man. I asked how he became interested in ships. As a young lad of sixteen, Theodore Cook sailed with his father and brothers on the sailing vessel *Ontario* for New York. He said that voyage was his first time at sea, and he was enthralled.

A day or so later the purser stopped in the passageway. He said "Sir, please allow me to compliment you for your ability to converse with our captain. I think if God almighty walked into the room my captain would simply say "Good day sir." I found Captain Cook to be a most interesting man. Born in England, he moved to America and then returned to England where he received his Master Merchant Mariner Certificate. He was intrigued by sailing vessels. I was interested in learning how running astern with a single propeller affects the control of the vessel. Capt. Cook asked how I controlled a sailing vessel without being able to shift to reverse. He had a very good reputation as an expert mariner. For his professional skill and dedication to the British Empire, Captain Cook was honored as a Commander of the Royal Victorian Order by Queen Victoria. He was a man of few words, but I enjoyed knowing him immensely. Save for a day of heavy seas which *Umbria* handled quite well, the trip was very enjoyable. But like any vacation as much fun as it was, it was good to be back home in the United States of America

51

ONE OF MY favorite weekend excursions was over to Greenwood Cemetery in the Kensington section of Brooklyn. Greenwood is a massive cemetery, some 475 acres. It was beautifully designed by David Bates Douglas. The Gothic main entrance on 25th Street looked like some of the buildings I saw in Europe. Nora said she had seen parrots perching on the spires. Annie and Robert loved the lake where they could feed the flock of beautiful white swans that were used to people and were very friendly. The cemetery began as a rural cemetery in 1838. Nora knew quite a lot about it because she was sometimes asked to sing at burials. She explained to us that the ground on which the cemetery was laid out was the scene of the Battle of Brooklyn during the American Revolutionary War. Greenwood is located between 20th Street to the northeast, Fifth Avenue to the northwest, 36th and 37th Streets to the southwest, Fort Hamilton Parkway to the south, and McDonald Ave to the east.

As I mentioned earlier, I have always been keenly interested in history and to this day have an extensive library of books accumulated from all over the world. I suppose it is natural, therefore, for me to be intrigued with Greenwood. Fortunately, Nora shared my interest, and Annie and Robert loved to visit. We would pack a picnic lunch, hook the surrey, and drive out to Greenwood for the day. The first stop always had to be the Sylvan Water Lake or Valley Water Lake so the kids could feed the swans the bread we had brought along for that purpose. I often visited the grave of Captain William Hayes, a man I knew. Captain Hayes was the master of the clipper ship *Rainbow* that was lost in 1848, only three years after her launching while rounding Cape Horn. There was another nautical-themed monument to Captain John Carreja. Anni used to call it "my daddy" because it was a figure of a ship's captain holding a sextant like the one, she had often played with in my office. For its stunning beauty and artistry, Nora loved the Morello-Volta mausoleum depicting a large-than-life bronze statue of a woman lying on a granite step and clutching a bouquet. Its light green patina made it all the more lovely. All the records of that mausoleum had been lost in a fire so there were only unconfirmed stories of its origin. One story said she had been shot by her former lover on the steps of a church on her wedding day. At the back of the base beneath a giant cross, there was the door that led to a stairway down into the crypt which contained a dozen caskets entombed in the walls. Nora was intrigued with an intricately carved monument that resembled a Gothic cathedral. Charlotte Canda was just 17 when she was killed---thrown from a runaway carriage when it overturned. Ironically, she had designed the monument for her recently deceased aunt.

Her father had her design constructed at very great expense, with added carvings of flowers, a star, and other decorations. Her distraught fiancé, a young nobleman named Charles Albert Jarret de la Marie committed suicide a year after her death and was interred just outside her plot. He was not allowed to be buried in her Catholic-consecrated plot. There was a massive monument that inspired me to visit the Erie Canal. Annie and John loved the story of Do-Hum-Me, the daughter of the Indian chief of the Sac tribe. P.T. Barnum had hired her and other Indians to perform wedding and war dances at his museum. Tragically just five weeks after she was married, she died from complications following a cold. The epitaph on her marble monument reads.

Thou art happy now for thou hast past
The cold dark journey to the grave
And in the land of light at last
joined the good, the fair, the brave.

The Brooklyn Fire Department had a whole section in Greenwood. Some of the sandstone tombstones were made in the shape of wooden fire hydrants. The gate was decorated with replicas of fire hosepipes, hooks and ladders, a parade torch, axes, and cast-iron hoses. In the center atop an obelisk-shaped monument stood a statue of a fire chief holding a voice trumpet in his right hand and on his left arm he is holding a rescued young child. Nearby there is another tall monument dedicated to "My Foster Mother." It was erected by a hero fireman named Harry Howard who had over one hundred rescues to his credit and was dedicated to the woman who adopted and raised him after she was saved from a burning building.

The statue my son Robert liked best was the drummer boy. Young Clarence Mackenzie was just 12 years old. He was a drummer boy with the 13th Regiment of the New York State Militia. Before he could ever get into battle he was accidentally shot and killed by another soldier during a drill practice. The lad was the first resident of Brooklyn to die in the Civil War. The statue depicts the Drummer Boy dressed in his uniform standing at parade rest holding his drum. The life-size statue is made of white zinc. Surrounding the monument are the graves of other Civil War dead.

One of my favorites was a monument dedicated to the souls lost when the first Clipper Ship *Rainbow* disappeared. *Rainbow* was assumed to be lost while rounding Cape Horn. It was to be Captain Hayes' last trip and both he and his wife were looking forward to his retirement. It was not to be. By November 2, 1848, the ship had not been heard from for 200 days. Nora walked away from that monument weeping. She said it brought back the fear she had endured when my ship sank, and I was feared to have been lost at sea after I had not been heard from for a year. I knew there was also an ornately carved monument to the *USM Artic,* sunk when she collided with the French vessel *Vesta* off Newfoundland in 1854. But I chose to avoid seeing the graphic depiction of the sinking ship for fear it would upset Nora. I do not think there ever was a time when we visited Greenwood that we did not discover a marvel we had never seen before.

52

⚓

THERE WERE OTHER excursions on the trip too numerous to mention here. I can say that we thoroughly enjoyed touring the Capitol and came away from the experience feeling proud to be Americans. The boat trip home was a much-needed rest and a pure delight. I considered myself blessed to have a wonderful family, good friends, a wonderful business, and some wonderful memories of my life at sea. I think the strong faith my parents instilled in me helped a great deal to get me through some difficult and dangerous situations at sea. My dad and my faith gave me a moral compass I steered by all of my life, well mostly. I know it made me a better captain in that I disavowed so much of the brutality associated with a sailors' life. I never ever ordered a man to be flogged. I never keel hauled anyone and I never ever would consider a cargo of slaves no matter how high the price. That did not mean I did not discipline my crew. I ran a tight ship, and sailors were punished fairly for their crimes and spent time in the brig if warranted. Getting to church was generally impossible when I was in the business of sailing but whenever I could, I attended church and took communion. When I gave up the sea Nora and I became regular church goers. We attended St. Josephs on Pacific Street.

My Annie grew to be a woman who sang beautifully like her mom and married a fine young man, Timothy Harrington, a civil engineer. He built a house on 60th Street in Mapleton Park in Brooklyn, so they were not too far away. They visited often. Annie loved horses and would spend hours in the barn behind our home pampering them. Timothy and I had some great chats over cigars and brandy. He was a smart well-educated fellow who enlightened me on the news of the day and what our new president Grover Cleveland was up too.

53

THEN IN THE summer of 1896, I was beginning to feel tired a lot and at times experienced pain in the right side of my abdomen. Nora noticed my discomfort and insisted I see a doctor. I was never big on going to doctors. Onboard ship we tried to use a commonsense approach to illness. And of course, we had our first aid and medical books. Finally, the pains and weakness were getting worse, so I agreed to see a doctor who had a practice just down the street. He did a lot of looking and testing, then sat me down in his office. He looked very serious. He said Mr. Sweeny you are a very sick man. You need to know that I will try everything I can to ease your pain with a medication called laudanum. But it is not a cure. He said honestly, I have little confidence that it will help. Perhaps if it gets too painful you could use some opium, He said, "I believe you have a disease of the liver that is exacerbated by your use of alcohol and tobacco. That demon in the decanter had done his work. I was shocked. I was 55 years old and in what I thought was pretty good health. The doctor suggested I get my affairs in order and hope for the best but plan for the worst.

Coel Pat Sweeny Portrait

Nora Sweeney

13th Cavalry Standard 2005

13th Cavalry Standard 2006

13th Cav Flank Marker 2003

13th Cav - Miller IV

Patrick Levi Sweeney 13th Regiment NY Cavalry

Patrick Sweeney's 13th Regiment issued a Smith and Wesson pistol.

Author's note. After a brief illness, Patrick Levi Sweeny died on October 10, 1896, at the age of 55 years. His wake was held in the couple's home on Pacific Street and lasted three days. The mayor of New York, several council members, clergy, and dignitaries attended. Friends and business associates, including the owners of the Bull Line and United Fruit Company attended. His body was transported to Holy Cross Cemetery in an ornate horse-drawn hearse preceded by two young boys dressed in black wearing high hats and carrying wooden staffs with black plumes attached to the top. His son Robert and his wife Nora arranged to have him buried in Holy Cross Cemetery in Brooklyn, New York. A handsomely decorated black granite monument was erected on the large family plot. Carved into the base in six-inch letters is the name Sweeney. There was room enough for the remains of his wife Nora, their immediate family including children John and Annie and Patrick's sister Bertha. And there was room too for future descendants of Captain Patrick and Nora Sweeny, including my mom Gertrude their granddaughter, and her husband, my dad Vincent Joseph Cerullo.

About the Author

BOB CERULLO

Over thirty years of experience as an auto mechanic/technician, service manager and automotive writer. Cerullo hosted the ABC talk radio network weekly Car Care Clinic for two years. He then switched to WOR Radio 710 where he fielded listeners car questions for several years as host of the AUTO SHOW. Cerullo provided weekly car care segments on the **Rambling with Gambling** program with both John A. Gambling and John R. Gambling. He has appeared numerous times on **The Dolans Smart Money** Radio Program, the Joan Hamburg Show, and Bernard Melzer programs on WOR Radio along with frequent appearances on WEVD Bernadette Michaels show. He was a guest expert on ABC Radio's Kathy Novack Show. The Owen Span program, Rich Taylor's Car Corner, and Talk Americas Auto World. Cerullo has been heard nationally in several radio markets with his Coping With Your Car Series.

Cerullo has provided his unique brand of easy-to-understand explanations of complicated automotive subjects on numerous TV shows including the **Late Night Show with David Letterman**. It was David Letterman who first nick named him THE CAR GUY He has appeared on **ABC Nightly News, Good Day New York**, **Good Morning America**, CBS TVs **Morning Show with Mory Alter**, CBS network TV, CNN-FNs Take It Personally, USA Live, Fox5 News, **The Maury Povitch Show**, CNBCs Smart Money Program, Channel 7 Eyewitness News, the CNBC Steals and Deals program, PBS TV, Cable visions You Auto Know Program, the Today Show and numerous CNBC special programs. He has done specials for Metro Guide and various Cablevision shows. Cerullo's informative TV segments have also appeared on the NBC TV Today program, and he was a regular featured guest on Channel 9 TVs Joe Franklin Show. Cerullo was the resident car expert on the Fox cable network FX Morning Breakfast Show, then on the Fox network After Breakfast Show, where he reviewed new cars and delivered car care information for drivers. Cerullo appears frequently on the Fox 5 TV Good Day New York TV program.

Cerullo has written feature stories on a regular basis for **PARADE MAGAZINE, AMI AUTO WORLD** Magazine and **MOTOR MAGAZINE**. He is the creator of MOTORS highly read TRADE SECRETS monthly column. He was a Jesse H. Neal Award finalist in 1999 and 2000. He has twice been awarded the International Automotive Media Medal in recognition of his excellence in automotive media. His articles in MOTOR MAGAZINE have drawn national attention when he exposed the counterfeit auto parts problem, focused industry attention on the hazards of asbestos in automotive brakes, and fraud in the periodic motor vehicle inspection programs across the country. His work on the dangers of Carbon Monoxide, Cell Phones, Road Rage, and Drowsy Drivers has won him national acclaim.

Cerullo's article: ARE YOU A RIPOFF MECHANIC? Alerted the automotive industry to its own dishonest practices and government efforts to stop them. Cerullo writes the UNDER THE HOOD column in each issue of AMI AUTO WORLD advising car owners how best to cope with their cars. His writing has appeared in AUTO WEEK, MOTOR SCOOP, PARADE MAGAZINE, VANTAGE, READERS DIGEST in both the national and international editions, POPULAR SCIENCE, THE POPULAR SCIENCE YEARBOOK, CONSTRUCTION CONTRACTING MAGAZINE, MEDICAL ECONOMICS, MONEYSWORTH, BROOKLYN BRIDGE MAGAZINE, AMI AUTO WORLD, NYFD magazine and others. Cerullo has delivered seminars at New York University, Brooklyn College and taught his AUTO MAINTENANCE 101 course at the Learning Annex in New York City for several years.

Cerullo has authored a book entitled: WHATS WRONG WITH MY CAR? Published by Penguin/plume, now in its fifth printing.

Cerullo is a graduate of Seton Hall University and was for over three decades, the owner/operator of an auto repair shop and diagnostic center in Brooklyn N.Y. He was named to the Mechanics Hall of Fame in 1977 along with famed race car mechanic George Bignotti. He is an affiliate member of the Society of Automotive Engineers, a former vice president of the International Motor Press Association and has been certified by the National Institute for Automotive Service Excellence (ASE). He is a member of the Board of Directors of the Service Technicians Society (STS). He has served to promote auto mechanic certification with the National Automotive Technician Certification board and has been a technical adviser to the Kings County District Attorney on automotive complaints. He has worked as a consultant to the New York Fire Dept. and is the owner/restorer of a prize-winning 1917 American La France fire engine now on loan to the NYC Fire Museum. Cerullo has received several awards for his educational work in the auto industry and consumer education.

Cerullo holds membership in SAE, STS, IMPA, and AFTRA. He served as an advanced life support EMT with the Deltaville Rescue Squad. He has written numerous articles for House and Home Magazine and LI Boating World Magazine. He is a licensed Merchant Marine Captain. Cerullo hosts radio programs on WWND103.9 FM radio.

Printed in the United States
by Baker & Taylor Publisher Services